ARE YOU CALLING ME BLACK?

by
Ojé's

Bloomington, IN  Milton Keynes, UK

authorHOUSE®

AuthorHouse™
1663 Liberty Drive, Suite 200
Bloomington, IN 47403
www.authorhouse.com
Phone: 1-800-839-8640

AuthorHouse™ UK Ltd.
500 Avebury Boulevard
Central Milton Keynes, MK9 2BE
www.authorhouse.co.uk
Phone: 08001974150

First published by AuthorHouse 11/22/2006

ISBN: 978-1-4259-6173-2 (sc)

CHAPTER ONE

I am somewhat mystified every time I hear the term "Black British", to my knowledge the cultural and behavioural make up of this sections of the community are so diverse it's virtually impossible to class these group of people together under one description. The issues around this group of people are so wide and diverse and sometimes so specific that to group together under one race is just wrong.

There are the Africans, then the Caribbean, then those born in Britain and have lived all their lives in England. Apart from the above group of people within the so called "Black British" there are sub divisions, within the Africans can be found several groups, north, west, and east Africans, all with different cultural make up. Africans and Afro Caribbean's are inherently different in everything they do, be it the criminal

1

activities they are involved in, study pattern, food they eat, how and where they live, cars they drive, the way they speak and general demeanour. Also within the Caribbean community can be found huge differences between the Jamaicans and the Dominican republics. Those born in England are not left out of the so called regional tags due to the fact that they are a make up of their parents, meaning, even though they have spent all their lives in England, they are tainted by their parents upbringing be it African or Caribbean. In the United States of America, people are referred to as Irish Americans, Italian Americans and so on and so forth, they are not all grouped together as European Americans, are they?

After years of trying to understand the so-called differences between the communities without much success, I decided to broach the subject among my group of friends. Oh, sorry, it seems I have been withering on without introducing myself; I am Adekunle Ademola Adegbite, suffice to say everyone calls me Ade! I am one of those individuals usually referred to as none descript; I am of average height, not skinny neither fat, clean-shaven sporting a little moustache on my upper lip. I am sometimes described as effeminate but apart from that I could easily disappear in a crowd. My group of friends are working youngish men (that's how they see themselves anyway), 35 to 39 years old, some married others still looking for that perfect partner and by that I mean someone prepared to sign a prenuptial or someone rich enough that they are comfortable in their own right. We are friends from university while one or two joined the group after we started our weekly outings. Let me introduce you to the group, there is me, Ade, Dave Wilkes, British born with Jamaican parents, Bharat Abhey, British born with Indian parents, he is generally called Baz and finally there is Abebe Abrafo, Ghanaian born, brought to England at a very tender age. We call him Abe.

We have been friends for about five years and we meet at our favourite wine bar called parks wine bar off Battersea park road. The location suits us all as it is in an easy place to get to. It's situated just off the main road with slight views of river Thames and the Battersea Bridge. The ambiance is that of a "living room" effect with easy chairs, not the usual leather sofas but posh looking three piece suites with matching single sitters and coffee tables, slow jazz or hip hop playing in the background with the occasional live visiting jazz quartet on hand. The furniture arrangement is augmented with the odd fish tanks dotted around the room with freshly picked flowerpots finishing off the whole picture. On the floor there is the very odd posh carpet, which totally throws you on entrance, as you don't expect to find that in a wine bar. Baz and I came across this little gem by mistake one hot afternoon while trying to escape from a persistent client. We basically ran into the nearest cosy joint we saw; that was three years ago. Now management consider the four of us regulars and part of the furniture as we are usually "parked" in our spot every Friday by 6.30. As explained, Baz and I work together, went to the same university, Middlesex, and we applied to the same company and luckily or unluckily depending on how I'm feeling about Baz at the time, were recruited at the same time through the companies graduate recruitment programme. The first time I saw Baz, there was one word that stuck in my mind, prim and proper. Baz was always well dressed, shirt neatly tucked into his trousers, belt stuck just below his belly button, shirt and trousers neatly ironed, hair placed strategically to the sides and back of his head. Baz was short, just below five foot, he was very light skinned for an Asian and without the black hair you could easily mistake him for a white man. We both studied finance and management and were lucky enough to be recruited by a bank. Prior to making friends with Baz at the university, there were preconceptions about Indian people and later he confirmed he had his preconceptions about black people as well. The funny thing was that he never realised

4

that there were huge differences between black people of African Descent and those of Caribbean Descent; to him black British were all the same. Anyways, I soon put him straight on that but I think in spite of all my explanations on our differences, it never really made sense to him until we made friends with Dave. Dave joined us at the company a couple of months after we had started, apparently he had been recruited same time as us but he was away visiting relatives in Jamaica and he had negotiated that into his start time at the company. Baz and I viewed him with much suspicion at the early stages as we were unsure how he was able to get away with starting later than the rest of us without him being tight with some high-powered manager at the company, thus making him a potential spy. Due to this misunderstanding, for the first couple of months at the company, poor Dave more or less spent by his lonesome self while we tried to figure him out. Also his look didn't help, he was a very tall huge man, even for a black guy, he must have been at least six foot five inches. His whole frame looked huge, huge shoulders, huge feet, huge hands and long legs that seemed to go on forever. To cap it all, when he spoke, his voice was so low, most people strained to hear him. The only thing that linked him to his Caribbean background was his long huge dreadlock hair; they were long and big, flowing all the way down to the small of his back. He toped up his look by spotting a pair of glasses, which looked incongruous on his massive face.

Going back three years ago, I am unsure who made the first contact between Dave and I, all I seem to remember is that we both came out of the coffee room at the office laughing hysterically at some joke we shared while the tea brewed. Suffice to say, as we ambled into the office, others gaped at us with mouths agape in wonder, thinking, Ade has defected to the other side. By this stage, our Friday evening slot was already on going, so I invited Dave along. Just as I was sitting down at my desk trying to take a sip of my brew, Baz tramps over, what were you doing chin wagging with the office misfit? I says to him, he is kind of an okay bloke, I invited him to join us at Parks this Friday, What! Shouts Baz, just leave it for now and we'll talk later. Baz skulks away, unhappy.

Abe, we met at a club in the west end. It was one of those night, you know the type, few women but loads of guys. It's so bad that the guys start to chat to each other just to commiserate on the lack of chicks on show. Baz and I spotted Abe standing all by himself against the bar, nursing a Mr Jack and coke, Baz and I enjoy Jack Daniels and coke so much we gave it our own unique name, Mr Jack. The club itself was nothing to write home about, the DJ was crap and so was the music. The place had the distinct feel of years of neglect and dirt. The carpet on the floor stuck to your shoes as you walked across it; so you had to raise your feet an inch higher just to move. The cubicles felt like there had been some lap dancing and other not so very nice things taking place there with the bar looking every inch as tired as the bartender serving behind it, you had the feeling that if you leaned too heavily on it, it could break into a thousand little pieces. The dance floor had a couple of girls who looked like they'd been there all their lives, the type that looked ready to drop their pants right there on the dance floor while the DJ shouted so much into the microphone, you couldn't hear a thing he was playing. The so called toilets felt like something you'd expect in a third world country with loos you couldn't flush, even if you tried all day. The regular toilet valet was more interested in selling you drugs than getting you to clean your hands after a good piss. The question would be, if you were sane, why oh why were you at this particular club on this particular night? Well, Baz and I were there to support an old struggling university colleague who was supposed to be playing that night. She went the "show business" route after university and was yet to break into the market, according to her she is in the process of "kissing her

7

frogs" prior to hitting the big time. We both hoped that was sooner rather than later as we were beginning to feel scared for her due to the clubs she gets to play in. Anyway, the clubs usually have the same theme, out in the middle of nowhere and usually she gets a mid week slot, like Wednesday or a Thursday. When she called to invite us to this gig, we had already decided we were not going, but when she explained the club was in the west end and she was playing on a Saturday night, we thought she was finally hitting the big time, whoopee doo daa, we could finally listen to our friend in a conducive environment without the worry of bodily harm or loss of limbs. Loo and behold we were faced with this god-awful place.

As we stood there transfixed on the whole set-up, our gaze came to rest on some fella stood by the bar who seemed to radiate the same uncomfortable feeling we were having. Baz and I said at the same time,

Bet you he was invited as well!

We stroll over to inquire about his story; he was very accommodating, which wasn't a surprise as he was on his tenth Mr Jack and coke. Apparently there was nothing else to do apart from drink, since the girls, club nor DJ did anything to lighten the spirit. To make matters worse, he was there to listen to the current DJ, who he knew had no talent but didn't have the heart to put him out of his misery. Abe looked like a typical African, short, stocky, broad frame and very dark. They must have invented the term "black" when they saw him, when he smiled in the club, all you saw were bright white teeth and two shinning eyes, that was it. He had a wide head that gave him a menacing look, the look of a boxer or a wrestler. When he laughed, it was like a mini explosion, everyone around turned to stare, which he never seemed to notice, he just carried on laughing. He talked in short spurts, very loudly like an automatic machine gun dispelling several rounds of bullets. We spent the best part of the night at the bar and then on leaving the club around five am, we exchanged phone numbers. Till this day, I'll never understand why we stayed at the club all night; it definitely wasn't for the girls or the music.

That's the gang, we try to discuss issues that are not potentially controversial or uncomfortable to anyone, there are a couple of subjects we do not discuss, for example, religion, world politics, girlfriends or wives, work, oh also we never ever talk about race issues. So you can imagine the shocked looks I got from my friends on this particular Friday, when out of the blue, while looking morosely into my fifth Mr Jack, I look up and say,

Why the hell do we all get classed as Black British?

There was about five minutes of uncomfortable silence from everyone. Baz, doing his usual best to avoid conflict, tried to diffuse the situation by cracking a joke.

Well, if you don't want to be called Black British, what do you want to be called, African Black British? You don't even know were bloody Africa is?

Well, my friend, that's where you are absolutely wrong, I spent the first five years of my life in London, was shipped to Nigeria, where I spent the next fifteen years.

My friends all looked at me with mouths dropping and shocked looks on their faces. It was as if they were seeing me for the first time.

CHAPTER 2

1972, Lagos Nigeria

Nigerian families based in England were just about accepting the fact that now might be a good time to go back to Nigeria, the civil war between the Igbo created Biafra state and Nigeria had just come to an end. The conflict, a result of ethnic and religious tension between the southern Igbo people and northern housas. Like most modern African nations, Nigeria was an artificial construct, put together by agreement between European powers, paying little regard to historical African boundaries or diverse cultural groups. The strange thing is that my early childhood recollection was when I was in Lagos, for the life of me; I couldn't remember anything of life prior to arriving in Nigeria. My big brother, who is three years older than me and more aware of his environment, told me everything of my life prior to Lagos. Thinking about it now, I guess life must have been so ordinary that it failed to make an impression on my tiny little mind. My parents, as was the norm of their generation, got sent to Britain to be educated. The idea being, they will then come back to Nigeria to input into the economy. As was the case in those days, every Nigerian going to Britain wanted to come to Nigeria to share in what was referred to as the "National Cake". The national cake being referred to was the oil. Nigeria struck oil in the late sixties and the economy had been booming ever since. Naira, the currency was exchanging at a rate of one naira to one pound, every western company worth its salt were jostling to get a foothold in the country. Nigerians were being exposed to things that were totally foreign to them, tarred roads, bridges, high rise buildings, chocolate, Uncle Ben's rice, cornflakes, foreign cars, television etc. To my knowledge, the first African television station was started in a town in Nigeria called Ibadan. Middleclass Nigerians, who had the chance, took to sending their kids to England to study, with the intention that on returning to Nigeria, they will be in a better position to take on the financial responsibility of the extended family. It should be mentioned that the extended family in those days could include 3 wives and 13 kids with uncles and aunties waiting in the wings. Usually, it worked out as expected, that is, the kids study in England, get a degree and return to Nigeria to help their parents. On the other hand, sometimes it didn't, some kids failed to return early enough, staying in excess of twenty years due to harsh reality faced in England during the sixties. This generation of Africans were thrust into a world they were totally unprepared for; there was the race issues, the extremely cold uncompromising weather, the hard graft, the loneliness, the lack of community and family support, coupled with the fact that they had to achieve an education within a specified amount of time all at the same time making financial provision to their parents back in Africa. Part of the problem faced by this generation of Africans in England was of their parents doing. On sending them to England, they made sure most of their kids went either as a couple or they were married in Nigeria prior to travelling to England with the promise, in blood, I might add, to send for their wives as soon as possible. This was done under the pretext that they didn't want their sons being "turned" by white women in England. What they failed to realise was that it was a fact of life that when you put a man and a woman together, in marriage as well, there tends to be kids following in tow sooner rather than later. This was an added complication not thought of. Nigerians in England, having to go to university and work at the same time to pay tuition, bills and money to Nigeria for family upkeep was very draining on this generation. Life was no bed of roses.

For as long as I can remember my parents, would look back on their days in England with both fondness and sadness and sometimes regret, based on what was being discussed. People have always wondered why there is so much rivalry between Caribbean and Africans, apart from the obvious issue of Africans being the perpetrators of selling Caribbean to the whites during the slave trade era, there is also the issue of my parents generation, who for as long as I can remember will always sit on their high horse and say things like, well, we were in England to study with the ultimate aim of returning to our country, while the Caribbean were in England just to build trains for the white folks and repair the damage caused to London due the second world war, in short terms, they were there to do manual labour. As I grew up and pondered this sentence, I kept wondering if my parents had any Caribbean friends all through their stay in England.

I think I was one of the lucky ones, my parents did complete their education, came back to Nigeria as expected after thirteen years with degrees under their belts and two kids in tow. Mum was a qualified nurse;

this was a good thing at a time when new hospitals were springing up in every nook and cranny, while dad was a qualified estate manager, also perfect for a country in the throes of rapid and furious development. Prior to returning to Nigeria, dad had arranged with some of his extended family for a nice house in a nice neighbourhood, that didn't happen. Our first house was in the slums of Surulere, a suburb in Lagos. On seeing the house, my dad was aghast, mum was reduced to tears but my brother and I looked on not really taking in what was happening. We moved in to a one-bedroom apartment on the second floor of a three-story house, fronted by a dusty clay road. The house itself had plastering peeling off, with what looked like a light shade of green as its original painting on the walls. There was no running water, neither was there electricity, apparently, NEPA, the national electric power authority had scheduled to install electricity the Friday prior to our arrival, yea right! The floors were concrete, with naked bulbs hanging off the ceilings, the doors had no handles or locks while the bathroom was downstairs in what can only be described as the lobby, so was the toilet and kitchen, all to be shared by others in the building. Along the narrow corridor from our apartment were three other families living in exactly the same type of apartment. As we were from England, we were given an extra room along the corridor, three doors from our main apartment. To get water, you had to go downstairs to the main courtyard, where there was a well. We were informed that this dried up regularly, so if you didn't want to be caught out, you stored several bucket loads in your apartment. To get to our street, you drove through dusty un-tarred roads, the nearest tarred road was the highway, 10 miles away.

I spent the first five years of my childhood waiting for my family's portion of the national cake. I just couldn't understand what we were doing living in such a run down hellhole, we were supposed to be middle class recently arrived from England. I guess as a kid, the priority for my parents wasn't to explain to me their plans, thus I carried on with life and made the best use of the situation. It wasn't all bad though, I did have some very life changing experiences that moulded me into the adult I am today. My first experiences as a child was trying to prove myself to the local kids, as a new arrival from England, which they somehow all knew, surprise! Surprise! The fact that I actually wore cloths and shoes had nothing to do with it. I was easy meat for anything and everything. I was supposed to be easy to "chance" which was a slang meaning easy to beat up on, easy to take sweets off, toys, exclude from games and generally slow on the up take. The first couple of months were routine, you woke up, got dressed, went to school, which was a stone's throw away, you came back home, had dinner, played with some toys and then went to bed. The only thing out of the ordinary was the dish being served. My parents were going back to their roots and so were only serving indigenous meals. I wasn't that bothered, but I can remember my brother complaining continuously at the dinner table about wanting fish and chips, bangers and mash and so on, chance would be a fine thing, in your dreams, matey. You get pap for breakfast, which was a sort of custard, yam and eggs for lunch and regular beans for dinner; I am not talking Heinz here! The highlight of the weekends was on Saturdays when we got served the local rice for lunch; this was made up of fifty percent rice, twenty five percent sand and twenty five percent stones. The long running debate was to determine who got the most stones in their meal.

Anyway, the fun really began a couple of months down the line when we had a mid term break at school. Seeing that I was cooped up at home all day, on one sunny afternoon, my mum says to me, Ade, why don't you go outside and play with the kids, I can hear them outside having fun. Mug, that I am, I heeded the advice and went outside, sheep to the slaughter. The first thing I notice is the dust around the kids, the next thing that jumps out is the attire, well, the lack of. There I was in my jeans, and a long jumper so as not to be bitten by insects, I had sandals with socks and to cap it all, I had gloves on to protect my hands from scrapes. I distinctly remember feeling I was dressed like an Eskimo at a Texan party, the kids, about a dozen of them, stared at me as if I was from Mars or something. Most of them hardly had anything on, it was pants (underwear) and that was it, no shoes, shirts or trousers. The pants could have been colourful at some point in their existence but after years of being used in the hot midday sunshine, through caked mud and grass, mostly, they looked like rags barely covering anything. This look was not retained only for the boys but also the girls, the only exception sometimes being that the girls had on singlet to cover the upper body. Well, there I was in my Christmas best and ready to join in the fun, that was before I understood what the fun games were. This group of kids, age five to eight, had a pre-set range of games due to the fact there were no toys, no park, swings, grass for footy, slides, basically nothing for kids to play on or with thus they made their own fun. Today, my first day out with the kids, I was introduced to a new form of football. This type of football involved the kids kicking anything and everything in sight along the dusty roads, and there were loads of stuff on the dusty roads, things like plastic bottles, used pack of cigarettes, sweets, dead animals and stones. The idea wasn't to pass or score or play from end to end, no, the idea was just to keep kicking until either the dead animal is totally and fully splattered all across the road or the packs or bottle gets to a place where no one can get to, this is usually an open pungent sewer running along the road. At the end of this game, the kids are covered not only in the dust, but also in cuts and bruises and splashes from whatever it was that was being kicked about. Alls I can say is that it was fun at the time.

I went home just after dinner time and my mum stood at the doorway with that look of "and who's stray kid are you and what have you done to my son?" on her face and I thought to myself, I must look exactly the same as the kids outside, result! By this time, I had lost my jumper, and shoes, the only thing I had on were my jeans. I had a nice time but at the expense of loosing most of my cloths and anything else in my pockets. There was a specific kid who took the lead in tormenting me, Segun; he was a particularly nasty piece of work. Short for his age, stocky, sores all over his arms and legs, ring worm on his cleanly shaven head. He had a habit of either poking his nose or digging at his scabs; he was permanently digging or picking at something. He took special delight in leading the pack of hungry wolves in tormenting the neighbourhood. He was the one who started the demand for my cloths. Arms akimbo, he stood in front of me on that faithful first day out and demanded he tried on my shoes due to the fact they looked like something he had previously owned. I later found out that the stance he took was a challenge, if I had stood up to him there and then, life would have been a lot easier. The following day, mum still went through the hassle of putting me in my Christmas best, same thing happened again; this time on my return home, I had only my pants on. On saying that though, I had loads of fun running around the neighbourhood catching or trying to catch grasshoppers. In and around the neighbourhood were little tuffs of bushes near some stagnant water where grasshoppers could be found. The general idea was to catch as many as possible in a tightly shut bottle; whoever gets the most grasshoppers is declared the winner. On declaration of the winner came the fun part, where you took out the insect's one at a time and removed their limbs one by one before finally squashing the defenceless insect, fun stuff.

I can't remember exactly when mum gave up the pretence of fitting me with a complete set of cloths, the fact that she kept on seeing kids on the street in my cloths didn't help, but all I remember is that the day came when on my way out to meet my friends, she made me wear a pair of shorts and that was it. No shoes, shirt or gloves. The years seemed to fly by, school, mid terms, games, growing up. There were several memorable times, like rolling a car tyre tube down the dusty road, renting bicycles and riding down the street, the best memory would be the goat fights. Each Christmas, it was tradition that all families would get a goat just for the festivities. Christmas was a very big deal; even those not able to afford one would somehow get one either via borrowing or buying on credit. This was a goldmine of opportunity for the kids, you could either play with the supposedly helpless things while they are tied to a tree, just before they realise they have horns as sharp as knives that could gourde you wide open with just one swift movement of their heads, or you could tease them by moving their feed just a few feet from their reach and watch them trying all their best to reach. Those little games didn't really fulfil the kids, no; maximum pleasure was derived by sneaking the hapless things to the fields, away from prying adult eyes very early in the morning. Each kid standing defiantly by their family goat boasting of its prowess as the strongest in the field, which could only be proven by each goat fighting each other until the last one standing. Many a goats died while this particular macho game went on, thereby plunging the affected families into despair during the festivities due to lack of food and after the festivities due to outstanding dept to be repaid on account of the goat. I will never forget when my goat died; I remember staying out all night, afraid to go home, knowing that my dad would be really angry. Finally got home around ten pm and got the beating of my life. Its funny, being beaten by your parents was a common thing, kids boasted of being beaten by their dads. It was an ongoing thing to compare notes and determine who got the most beating in a week. Sometimes, due to the fact that the dads were hardly around, the communication you had with your dad was when he was belting you or physically throwing you across the room for something you did. As a kid you felt closer to your dad, you knew you did something terrible and he cared enough to spare the time to give you a very good hiding. I should point out that after my beating; I never took our family goat for fights again.

By this time there were wide ranging changes taking place in Nigeria, it seemed over night all roads leading to our house got tarred, we had electricity in the house and running water. All this while, unknown to me, my dad was working with the central Government in building a flagship town in Lagos for a pan African festivity to be held in Nigeria, called FESTAC. At the end of the function, certain workers were given properties at the flagship town for services rendered and as a sort of company house. We moved in to festac in 1977. I must confess that my memory of England was by now non-existent especially after spending the last five years in Surulere. My first view of Festac left me gobsmarked, tarred roads, street lights, traffic lights, zebra crossings, shopping malls, parks, terraced houses, front gardens, back gardens, driveways, standby generators to counter the irregular national electricity, named closes and roads. This must be England, it was a far cry from my old neighbourhood, it was another world entirely, a world I felt I belonged. Living in festac was a different ball game entirely, there were no kids hanging around outside, in fact you hardly saw anyone outside, people went from their front doors straight into their cars barely pausing to say hello. You could hear kids playing in their gardens, but never outside, which was very difficult for me to get used to. The more I stayed in doors, the more I got interested in television, novels, music and comic books; there was a huge supply from the nearby library. This was a whole new type of lifestyle for me, which I must say definitely improved my education and my knowledge; it probably didn't do anything for my people interaction skills.

I was just about the right age to start secondary school, was beginning to understand adult conversations about the Government, the economy, tribalism, bribery and corruption, religion and every other issue supposedly pulling the country apart. At this stage, the country was bundling from one military dictatorship to another, with each military leader doing as much damage to the economy as they possibly could. Things were looking better at home though, dad, it seemed was getting paid more and the same thing was happening to mum. I think by now, the old folks were getting pretty disenfranchised by the local menu; we seemed to be reverting back to their favourite meals when they were in England. There were the usual stuff for breakfast, cereals; lunch sometimes included potatoes while dinner could sometimes be baked beans and toast. It was as if they were trying to forget all that going indigenous crap and return to what they've been used to during their thirteen years sojourn in England. They were in a very uncertain place. Should they carry on as the dedicated Nigerians, ready to serve their country no matter what, even in the face of unfairness and lifestyle which was very unaccommodating when not part of the ruling cliché or return to a life in England which they had come to love and was now sourly missed, catch twenty two situation. If they gave up and went back to England, like so many of their colleagues were doing, they would feel a failure in their own country but on the other hand, if they stayed, the idea of the type of lifestyle to expect wasn't all that except they embraced the lifestyle of the country, this was a conundrum as they couldn't bring themselves to take up this lifestyle. A lifestyle where you had to bribe someone to do their job, a life where, if you expected to make something of yourself, you had to ingratiate yourself to some uneducated military personnel, a life where you could be shot by a roadside policeman or corporal, a life where buglers would inform you that they were coming to your house on a certain day, be ready. The country was fast heading down the tubes for some people while others were raking in the money and living like kings and queens. When it came down to it, they were trapped, the extended family, the idea of going to start all over again in England, the thought of having to leave their aged parents alone in Nigeria was just too much of a sacrifice. So unlike so many of their generation who couldn't re-integrate into the society, they stayed, to their detriment.

Nigeria at this stage was for either the fast or the slow, there was a saying then, "if you slow, you blow", which basically meant, you either got with the programme or you were left way behind on the scrap heap. If you had a conscience, leave. Sadly, both my parents had a conscience, which meant they survived only on their salary and missed out on the free flowing money of the time. Successive military Governments made money available to the crooked and connected people, especially if you were educated; contracts were awarded for jobs that never took place, monies shared between the contractor and the Government official awarding the contract. Large sums of money exchanged hands with no visible work being undertaken. Secondary school was definitely an education, you learned about the history of the country, about jaja of opobo, the caliphates, Yoruba, Hausa and Igbo. You read books by Wole Soyinka, Chinu Achebe and Shakespeare all in the same vein. Education was a mixture of Nigerian culture and history with a tint of the old colonial masters, British. You were exposed to the greatness of the country and the gradual fall into the white colonials, then the gradual re-education into western worlds with warring caliphates brought together under countries that could never in a million years live in peace together. I always wondered in later years why we were never exposed to the history of slavery. You learned of those who fought for independence from the colonial powers, how Africa was then found to be a land full of natural resources like gold, oil, silver and diamonds which eventually brought back all the old colonial masters as conglomerates, which then lead to the loss of structure and culture. There were widespread breakdown of cultures, with people migrating to inner cities in search of their fortunes, which lead to slums and high rate of poverty.

By this time, my family had gone full circle, poverty, educated, upper middleclass, lower middleclass and then breadline surviving. The cereals were the first to go, then the potatoes and baked beans. In a twinkle of an eye, we were back to the menu we got used while living in Surulere. Festac was fast becoming a town where everyone and anyone wanted to live, thus the structure was fast dissipating, parks were being converted to houses, roads were no longer being maintained, full of potholes, traffic lights were no longer working, street lights the same, generators were being stolen and sold off on the black market. Festac in truth was fast becoming a Surulere, as was the rest of Lagos. The level of dirt in Lagos was so bad that the Government introduced a programme called "Operation Clean the Nation" to get rid of the filth. This was one of many programmes by as many military dictators. Another issue at the time was the rowdiness of people, people not willing to wait their turn or parking their cars in the middle of a highway to chat or fight while holding up the traffic, driving the wrong way just to beat the traffic, it got to a point where one of the many military leaders introduced a programme to clean up the attitude called "war against indiscipline". This could only happen under military rule, the idea was on being caught throwing litter on the floor, you were punished by military personnel, and this could include but not preclude flogging, kneeling in the streets with your hands in the air, even if you had a suit on, frog jumping or lying face down in the mud for your sins. Anyone caught "jumping a queue" faced the same treatment. Life was generally hard for some and rosy for others, the favourite saying was "no condition is permanent" due to the fact that the minute you fell out with your cliché, you were left high and dry with nothing.

By the mid eighties, my parents had decided that my brother and I would return to England, they came to realise that things were only going to get worse in Nigeria.

CHAPTER 3

Parks wine bar was fast filling up with the usual clientele, as it was getting noisier and more difficult to get the attention of the waiters. The clientele was very mixed, youngish and middle age, whites, blacks and Asians. The evening clientele were a bit different to the afternoon clientele in that they were not all city workers or necessarily worked at all, while the afternoon clientele were definitely the city boys and gals treating their clients to a good meal and some hard liquor trying to make them more amenable or receptive to sales pitch. Abe grunted under his breath something about how the bar kept the chairs clean as they were not leather and how they kept changing the patterns and oh, why or why did they keep carpets on the floor rather than the usual wooden floors that was the norm in every other wine bar in the neighbourhood. Will that be your feeble effort at changing the subject? Says I, well, to answer your question, the chairs have covers, which are replaced everyday, the carpets on the floor would be the bar's way of saying we are different, guys, we've been friends for ages; we should have reached a place where we can have a serious conversation about issues around us, especially as it affects everyone at this table. I personally know for a fact that in spite of me being born British, some of my values are defined by my spell in Nigeria, which may or may not prejudice me towards certain issues in relation to my fellow black British brothers. For example, it has always been the case that British African's feel Caribbean are unnecessarily aggressive towards them due to the fact that they felt betrayed by their African brothers who sold them into slavery, I would like to discuss that particular myth. I am sure that you guys have other influences in your life that sometimes leads to friction that you are unaware of or unwilling to accept.

Well, if we are to discuss such issues, shouldn't we at least get rid of Baz? Abe interjected.

I notice Dave starring into his half empty Mr Jack, not uttering a word, Dave, what have you got to say to my last statement, is it true or not?

I think I need another Mr Jack, double, before I can discuss anything of importance, but in the meantime, I do agree with Abe, Baz isn't black, so we shouldn't be discussing this in his presence, Dave replies.

All the while, I could see Baz getting agitated and squirming slightly in his comfortable chair.

Asians are black, in case you don't know, Baz finally chips in,

How and when, Dave counters, when it suites you guys, or when you reckon you need a bit of black support to achieve an aim and once the aim is achieved, revert back to type and deny us?

Is that what you think Asians do? Asked Baz?

You bet your ass, countered Dave.

Baz has a sharp intake of breath, gazes around the table at his group of friends who do not seem to have any idea about his background, let alone what has shaped him into the man he is today.

Guys, you should never take on face value what you see, especially with people of ethnic minority, what you see isn't necessarily what you get, there are usually different facets to these people, as you should all know. I am definitely a city boy and I will, if needed pass myself off as either black or Asian, depending on the situation I find myself. Do you know why this is? Well, it's to do with the issues we faced so many years ago, both in England and back at home in India or Pakistan. I was obviously brought up by my parents

31

who grew up in the mean streets of Calcutta and I have unknowingly imbibed some of their values, good or bad. I do mix with other Asians and I am aware of the sometimes-fragile relationship between the very young Asians and black kids. This is born out of a need for them to assert themselves after so many years in Britain of being known as docile and not troublesome. Young Asian kids, not like I am saying I am no longer young, but we are talking teenagers here, feel a need to carve out their own identity rather than carry on with those of their parents, you all know what I mean. The idea that Asians are in England to either open a curry shop, a corner shop or "Sari" shop or work all the hours god sent just to make enough money to eat. Not wanting to be seen or heard, but just to be left alone to their devices so they can quietly carry on with their lives. These kids witnessed the injustice being meted out to their Asian brothers due to the fact that they are not as loud as the Blacks, so they made a decision that if it takes a loud person to achieve their needs, then they'll be loud. You need to realize that my generation of Asians grew up with whole different set of values; this was due to the fact that our parents had us just as they arrived in England and they still had all the baggage from India or Pakistan.

1962, Calcutta, India

Sobur Abhey, was born in Calcutta, he made his living through his cleaning business providing cleaning service to the native upper class, British, mixed race, white people or rich in Calcutta. He would clean any homes, offices or animals used for either transport or sport. These could include elephants, horses, donkeys and sometimes-ceremonial cows. As part of his cleaning business, he also picked up the art of ceremonial decoration of animals for grand ceremonies or entertainment.

He lived in the slums of Tollyguni with his parents who had been around during the torrid times in Calcutta. Calcutta is a city reflecting its colonial past, industrial decline and hopeful resurgence in its near future. After independence from the British colonials in 1947, when the country got partitioned between India and Pakistan, Calcutta was included in the Indian part of Bengal, West Bengal. Calcutta became the capital city of the state of West Bengal. This was another example of the colonials bringing together a group of people as one state who under normal circumstances, could not interrelate in whatever form or shape. There was religious strife, which led to migration of Hindus from the newly formed East Pakistan to the city. With the achievement of independence, the divisions of the colonial city sourly remembered by Sobur's parents were retained. Native upper class now occupied the privileged areas reserved for the colonizers. The population were at best being accommodating rather then intimate, which was not helped by the political climate. The centrist, leftist and radical forces fought for control of the state which led to a succession of coalition governments unable to bring calm or confidence to the city. There was also migration into the city due to the India-China war, thereby making the city a boiling pot of submerged feelings ready to explode. Tollyguni was known for its infrastructure deficiencies, absence of planning evident in the congested lanes, open drainage, very congested living conditions. Segregation was rampant; it could be by religion, caste, occupation or ethnicity. As a low caste Hindu, the Abhey family had painstakingly kept a low profile, going about their business quietly without causing any unnecessary attraction. The current issues unfolding in Calcutta were of little interest to Sobur, as his sole ambition was to make as much money as possible to live in the posh areas of Calcutta like Burrabazaar. He was content to bide his time and salt as much of his money away as possible. Sobur's plans went out the window one sunny dusty afternoon in Burrabazaar.

As a form of inspiration, Sobur travels to the posh areas around Calcutta to impress on himself the reason why he needs to work hard to make something of himself. He would enjoy sitting around watching the rich live out their days, interested in how they spent their time and days. He also took it upon himself to personally carry out any cleaning for clients from these places, like the areas around the lakes and south Calcutta. On the faithful day that would turn his life upside down, he walked along the streets watching people going by, taking in the atmosphere, trying to imagine himself having the same type of lifestyle, being able to classify himself as a self made entrepreneur in the same vein as the Marwaris. Right before him was this beautiful white house with well tended gardens and lawn, front men could be seen scurrying around trying to get things in order ready for the master of the house. The front entrance was large with pebbled driveway, leading up to front porch of huge four pillars holding up a massive balcony. On the balcony, wearing flowing white gown, veil and sandals, was a slender built woman, looking ahead forlornly as if in waiting for some rescuer. His first impression was, another rich little daddy's girl, bored out of her brains looking for some servant to torment, but then she removed her veil due to the fact that a front man called up to her, Eshal, you shouldn't be out there, your mum will be back soon and so will your dad, you know they will not be pleased. Do you want me to bring you anything? Sobur stood there transfixed as he watched her open her mouth to answer the front man, she looked like a goddess, for an Asian, she was very light skinned, almost white, long flowing dark hair, shining brightly in the midday sun, eyes, almost as clear as the sky, with a hint of colour. She had the look of someone pained to be there, almost apologetic to the front man, which at the time, Sobur thought odd. He was sucker punched by a thunderbolt! This woman will be his wife.

He later found out that the family were part of the business elite, who made their money from the industrialized Calcutta but have now diversified into politics. Mr Ahmed is part of the leftist fighting for control of the state. The daughter, Eshal, is currently betrothed to a political friend of the Ahmed's; apparently this was a political union, nothing more. It was designed to increase the leftist hold on the state. Poor Eshal had no say in the matter. When Sobur told his father of his love for Eshal, he was advised to forget her and carry on with his life, what are the odds that a union would be allowed between people of different class, caste, wealth and religion? The fact that she is Muslim and you are

Hindu totally nullifies the idea of it ever taking place. The sixties Calcutta frowned heavily upon marriage between different caste, they strongly believed every one should stay within their own caste and not integrate in any way due to the fact that this will lead to caste dilution.

In spite of all the barriers against him, Sobur was determined to win Eshal's heart; he also truly believed she was looking for true love rather than the arranged marriage she was headed for. He got himself on the staff of the Ahmed's and after months of trying hard to get her attention, he finally got it at a very embarrassing time. She was parading in her room, showing off a new attire bought her by her dad when she caught sight of him at the door and she apologised and inquired what he wanted. Without realising, he blurted out his love for her, he explained that he had been in love with her since the first day he saw her, which was five to six months ago,

But I know you, you have just joined my father's staff, how can it be that you have been in love with me for over five months, Eshal inquired?

I only joined the staff to be closer to you, I saw you standing on your balcony and fell in love with you.

Eshal was embarrassed and didn't really think he was serious, so she waves him away and carries on

37

examining herself in the mirror. Sobur carried on at Eshal for another four months before she started taking him seriously and they would sneak hours and hours of conversation together anywhere around the house where discovery was virtually impossible. They talked about him and what he did, she was surprised that he had the time to put in a full days work at her father's house and still have the time to keep an eye on his business and workers. She wondered if due to the fact that he wasn't there if he was loosing money, he agreed but pointed out that he would do anything for the woman who would be his wife. She pointed out to him the fact that they were from different backgrounds and that she was already betrothed to a very wealthy and jealous politician who would stop at nothing to get rid of both of them if there was even a whiff of anything happening to tarnish his image.

Calcutta was going through a torrid time, it was 1972 and there was tension due to the India-Pakistan war on freedom of Bangladesh, the Naxalite movement hit the city resulting in arrests of hundreds of youths and creating more tension among the dwellers. There were deep divide between the natives and their upper class and white residence, mainly due to the divide in living standards. The upper middle class lived in areas labelled as "European towns" characterised by spacious bungalows, elegant houses, planned streets, recreational areas reserved for Western recreational facilities such as race, and golf courses, soccer and cricket. While in the native town, the opposite was the case; these were poorly serviced and highly congested. A survey was carried out on pavement dwellers in 1971 during the census in India, which found out that about 50 thousand homeless persons in the Calcutta's rich and affluent places, but the level of pavement dwellers was non existent in the slums. This brought to the forefront the level of divide in the city. As the city went from crisis to crisis, Sobur was having a personal crisis that would change his life forever. Eshal became pregnant with his baby. After months of deliberating a way out of their predicament, they finally agreed that to stay in Calcutta would be harmful not just to them but also to their families and their unborn child; it would be safer for everyone concerned if they disappeared out of the country. They thought of relocating to another city but soon ruled that out as soon as it became clear that the politician Eshal was betrothed to had contacts in every nook and cranny of India, he would find them and hurt them. England was the logical option. Sobur sold his business, said his goodbyes to his parents, met up with Eshal at the airport, by now she was partly showing, if you looked hard enough. A wise old woman told them that Eshal was having a boy; they decided to name him Bharat. They left Calcutta without much regret, as they could finally be together without the stigma of bringing shame to anyone around them.

CHAPTER 4

The waiter comes round, as he usually does with a tray full of three Mr Jacks and a beer. Abe, Baz and I drink Mr Jack while Dave is a beer man; he reckons hard liquor will damage his kidneys, so he won't touch the stuff. He will however drink more than the rest of us and also get drunk faster than the rest of us. Its about seven pm at Parks wine bar, the music makes a further descent in sound by an octave, with love crooners like Barry White, Luther Vandross and Lionel Ritchie taking centre stage, the lights become dimmer as the bar re-aligns itself to another type of ambiance, usually for lovers wanting to cuddle up in any of the easy chairs for a kiss and a cuddle. The bar did however provide table lamps for each set of chairs wanting to make the area brighter, especially if the romance wasn't blossoming or in our case you are with friends that you are not necessarily inclined to want to have a kiss and cuddle with. There are shades on the windows that are electronically released to block out the street lights, the huge plasma screen television was usually on mute, and on a music channel, rather than Sky sports, there are candles littered around the place which go off systematically one at a time to make the place just that little bit dimmer creating the effect of cosy living room setting. Anyways, after Baz's tirade, we were avoiding eye contact with each other and not in a hurry to switch on the table lamp, the drinks got passed around and we sat there for about five minutes just sipping, lost in our own private thoughts, each person engrossed with sipping and or stroking their individual drinks.

Oi, man, put on the bloody light, don't want people getting the wrong idea about us, shouts Abe to Dave, who was sat right beside the table lamp.

Dave, reluctantly reaches out to turn on the light, you could see everyone shifting uncomfortably in their sits trying their best not to appear uncomfortable, everyone avoiding looking in Baz's direction.

Baz broke the silence, look, guys, its quite obvious that as an Asian, I am not black but the reality is that most of the things that makes you guys feel black, has happened to Asian's as well. Take racism, colonisation, slavery, poverty, inequality and so on, I could go on all day, these are the things that defines a black person, these things may not have happened directly to most of us sitting here, but we have experienced the effects through our parents, our grand parents, friends, relatives and via the media. True, as Asians we sometimes can escape some of these ills of society but not entirely, and when we do come across a great injustice due to the fact that we have a different skin colour to others, we will try and identify with others who surfer the same fate. The issue of Asian's sometimes trying not to identify with blacks is just human behaviour, which is manifested between African and Caribbean blacks as well. I have been a friend to Ade, going on five years, I have spent time with his family and friends and it never ceases to amaze me the similarities in cause and effect of an instance. Anytime I am in the presence of his African friends and we just happen to be listening to the news, a news item comes up saying something about a murder, a mugger or a car thief, there is complete assurance among these group of people that if the person being accused is a black man, no way will he be of African origin, or am I wrong, Ade?

Well now that you mention it, we do not do stuff like that, its just not us, I answer, but on the other hand, if there is a news item about forgery, fraud, con artist, well that's another matter, usually we are surprised if the culprit is not of African origin.

So there you go, said Baz, that's human nature to want to identify with the good but extricating yourself from the bad aspects and it doesn't make Asian's any less black. Have you guys never wondered how I feel when we talk about football, do you guys not think it absurd there not being a single Asian player in the premiership? That, to my knowledge will be Asian's still suffering racism.

Now hold up, that is an entirely different ball game, excuse the pun, you guys must suck at playing footy, says Dave, and the issue of certain types of Blacks being the sole perpetrators of certain unlawful practices is just rubbish. Loads of blacks are good footballers and loads of blacks manage teams, but none are managers in the premiership, you don't hear us whinging about it, do you?

Well, I think I must agree with that assertion, says Abe, very rarely will you find a black British of African origin being involved in any criminal activity requiring physical energy, inherently, we are better at using our brain power rather than grunt. What are you implying? Asks Dave, are you saying that you guys have more brains than us?

No, but I am saying that we did use a lot of brawn in the past only to find out that you do not necessarily achieve the maximum you can that way, but on the other hand, using your brain power gets you a whole load more, not saying that you guys haven't yet figured that one out or anything, but it seems rather than put in the initial hard graft needed for being able to use your brain power, you guys would rather be out on the streets earning pittance. Let's face it; we all went to university here, the ratio of blacks to Asian's to whites was just unbelievable. Now among the blacks, the ratio of those from Caribbean origin was so minuet, it was embarrassing.

Well, did it ever cross your mind that it could have been due to the fact that university was too expensive?

Ah, give me a break, shouts Abe, that was never the case, we know how much it cost to attend uni and how much help we received from the state and the dept we owe, that was never the issue, Dave, admit it, a huge percentage of you guys do not believe in education, which is why a huge percent ends up being involved in illegal activities. Abe, any more talk from you and I will have to come over there and thump you in the face, now, will you give me a chance to defend my case?

Right! I want to go on record to say that whatever the statistic say or the media, we are not all drug pushers and state benefit dependents or "baby fathers" as so widely publicised, there are great scholars from the West Indies, take my family for example, I have three sisters and cousins who are qualified accountants, lawyers and engineers, they were mostly educated in Jamaica prior to coming over to England. Most of our friends and extended family are educated and earning money legally rather than illegally. As you know I was born here but my sister weren't, and I must admit that the reasons for lots of people not bothering to attend uni is nothing to do with experience back in the West Indies but more to do with what their parents and grand parents went through when they came to England. As Ade rightly said, lots came to England during the time just after the war when there was a shortage of labour; it was down to them to put a new infrastructure in place. So when these generation of people keep banging on about the sacrifices they made, their children are not impressed due to the fact that they were still treated dismally after all their sacrifices for the country. This has lead loads to believe that now is a time to reap what their parents and grand parents have sowed rather than grafting themselves but that is still a very small percentage. The greater percentage of Caribbean do believe in education, they do believe in a honest days work for a honest days pay, the problem we have here is that if our fellow black British here, around this table still questions our motives and lifestyle, then we are all doomed. What you all fail to realise here is that the common person on the streets of England is unable to differentiate between an African British and one from the West Indies; we are all tainted with the same brush. Rather than joining the bandwagon, shouldn't we here around the table try to understand the cause and effect?

Okay, Dave, will you enlighten us as to the cause of your predicament, which in your words is our predicament as well? Abe Said.

Dave had a look of disappointment on his face as he surveyed the table; he had hoped he had a group of friends who were more enlightened now realising this was not the case was quite demoralising discovering his friends had the inherent misconceptions about Caribbean. He was trying to gauge if it was worth his energy in trying to enlighten this bunch, but saying that, he did have his pre-conceptions about Asian's as well, having preconceptions was just human, it couldn't be helped, perhaps he shouldn't be so judgemental.

You know what? I need to take a piss, you guys can carry on without me and I am not sure I can be bothered to enlighten you and with that, Dave goes off in a huff, heading towards the loos. Abe gets up,

I think I'll join him, this discussion is getting too serious for my taste; while we are gone, please think of something less provocative as a discussion topic as you are putting me off my relaxing drink.

Baz and I were left to our own devices, I look at Baz and he is close to giving up as well, but I personally think we are making progress as a group of friends for a change in our lives. For once we are able to discuss issues that affect us on a daily basis without reverting to irrelevant chitchat. I think if we can get past these initial feelings of being individually attacked, which to me should have happened at the early stages of our friendship and then we would come to understand better our issues and be in a better position to discuss issues when they are raised against black British.

Baz, you don't really believe that crap you just spewed a few moments ago, do you, you being black and all?

He looks at me with a cheeky grin on his face,

What do you think?

Hey, man, if you are happy to be classed as white, that's your problem, you don't have to pretend with me you know.

Baz jumps up from his sit and practically screams at me, I knew you didn't believe, you know something,

I think you are the racist person here, I'm off home and I'll see you tomorrow in the office.

Baz, will you pipe down, I was just trying to gauge your sincerity, I for one have never seen you talk so passionately about issues affecting black British and the fact that you class yourself as part of that group, was, to be frank, a surprise to me. Sit down man and stop being a baby, will you get the waiter to come over while you are up there, I'm gasping. Baz sits down reluctantly with a suspicious look on his face, while at the same time signalling for the waiter.

But what do you think of all this though? Do you think Dave is right, that we need to accept all our issues in totality rather than piecemeal as it relates to each race within the black community? I ask, he does have a point, if we are divided even amongst ourselves, how the hell will we argue against those trying to pigeonhole us,

Baz responds, but I thought that was the whole point, its our diversity that suggest we shouldn't all be tagged with the same "Black British" label. I'm lost, Baz says, and I need a drink, where is the waiter?

Ah. There you are, thanks, Baz says to the waiter, are you keeping an eye on the bill and our limit? We do have a tab for the day but we also have an agreed limit, so please keep an eye on it as you are bringing the drinks.

Abe and Dave return to the table in animated discussion, Abe, gesticulating furiously, trying to make a point.

What's the topic of conversation, ask Baz?

Well, says Dave, Abe here believes we need to discuss where mixed race people fit into our discussions.

My gut feeling is that it depends on the individual, says I, those who feel black are black and those who feel white are white, simple.

Dave responds, nah mate, it ain't that simple you know, some mixed race kids are mixed up in the head about their race due to their parents influences in their lives, its not down to them you know. Parents sometime pass on their baggage onto their kids; take for instance a parent who had an interracial relationship, when one partner leaves, leaving the other to bring up a kid as a lone parent, the parent left holding the baby, literarily, won't be too forthcoming in extolling the virtues of their missing black or white partner. Nah, they'll be going out of their way to point the kid towards being white or black and staying away from the other race.

Okay, we have mixed race black British who are black and those who aren't, so what to do about those who don't want to be referred to as black, says Abe, well, my understanding is that we have enough problems trying to understand the issues with those who want to be black so best not to complicate the issue by trying to persuade those who don't want to be. It will be ideal for all concerned that those with identity issues or crisis are left to work out their own race issues and then welcome them into the fold if and when they decide they are comfortable enough with themselves to be called black anything.

Baz interjected jokingly, you know, the swinging sixties has a lot to answer for, what with the issues created in the Caribbean community, the Asian community and now the mixed race community, which as far as I am aware all started during that era.

I agree, all the issues currently being suffered by the Caribbean community definitely started during the swinging sixties, Dave said, for as long as I can remember, my mum and dad could trace everything to that era.

CHAPTER 5

1960, London, England

The swinging sixties, fondly remembered by all those who were present at the time as a time of free love, youthful exuberance, infertile radicalism and pop music, the Beatles reigned supreme. London was characterised by the blitz of World War II, the bombing by the Germans, killed at least 30,000 Londoners and flattened residential and public houses and other historical buildings, the rebuilding was a mixture of differing architectural styles thus resulting in the lack of unity in architecture which was now part of London's charm. Residents used to war rations were now exuberating in the experience of newfound freedom of choice of food, clothing, social functions and entertainment. The sexy way in which the sixties is remembered never seems to take into account the experience of the ethnic minorities of the same era, minorities like black Africans, Caribbean's, Irish, eastern Europeans or Jews. In post war London, the demographics changed due to immigration from the British old empire, Nottinghill and Brixton acquired a large Caribbean population, Hong Kong immigrants settled in Soho, Sikhs in Southall and Cypriots in Finsbury. Their experiences of that era aren't something that is remembered that fondly; it was one of constant daily struggle for survival, open racism, alienation and segregation. The early Caribbean migrants who came off the windrush voyage at Tilbury in 1948 had gone through several riots in 1958 in Nottinghill, Liverpool and Oldham. Don't get me wrong, it wasn't all bad, but it wasn't as good for minorities as constantly depicted in the history books. In the United States of America where the same situation occurred, they had the benefit of religion, music and national personalities in the form of Martin Luther King and Malcolm X to pin their hopes on for some sort of emancipation, in England, there was no such luxury. The Africans were mostly concerned and worried about their home countries and being free from colonisation and the dream of returning to a free country while the Caribbean's were more concerned about settling down and making a living, providing for their families.

Dennard Wilkes and his wife Mia settled in a little one bedroom flat in Santly Street in Brixton, they had their three daughters, Abigail, Maurita and Ayana living in residence as well. The Wilkes had planned not to have any more kids, especially due to the cramped nature of their current accommodation. They were thankful for getting a place to stay after months of searching, the process of searching for accommodation itself was very demoralising, it was common to be turned away by landlords on the pretext that others wouldn't like sharing a house with coloureds as they were referred to. The Wilkes were unsure which situation was worse, the one where there is a sign on the door saying "no coloured, Jews, Irish or dogs welcomed" or the situation where there was no sign but on knocking on the door you were given an excuse about current residents not wanting to share, nothing to do with the landlord not wanting you. Dennard and Mia were the second black family to move into the neighbourhood, which initially had mainly polish and Jews in residence. The racial fallout of a second black family moving into the neighbourhood was unexpected by the Wilkes family, it seemed the original settlers were content when it was just the one black family in the neighbourhood but as soon as a second family moved in, they are up in arms. Most residents were working classes with a few middleclass languishing in the neighbourhood looking to move upper, higher and away from this working class region. Dennard noticed that the working class were the most vocal in their condemnation of the new black family, they were the aggressive ones on the street, they were the ones who threatened his daughters to stay away from their sons, they were the ones who kept a keen eye on the black men in the streets, just to make sure that the forbidden love between a black man and a white woman didn't take place. Dennard made it a point to keep his family in doors as much as possible and on the odd occasion when they had to go out, they were all together or in groups. Mia made overtures to the other black family on the street, at first they were happy to see another black family and they welcomed Mia into their house but when they faced the fallout from their former friends, they too withdrew their friendship. The whole situation was very hard on Mia, since she came from a middleclass Jamaican family, this was her first experience of segregation and she was constantly depressed and unable to go anywhere. Mia was a fragile woman with a very fragile frame; she was five foot, slim built, long dark hair, very fair and sometimes pale for a black woman. Her movements were slow and premeditated, she never seemed to do anything spontaneously and it seemed every movement was thought of deeply. She is unassuming and unobtrusive, preferring her own company most of the time. After the first couple of months, Mia was not copping any better with the whole situation, Dennard after discussion with relatives and friends had decided that it may be better for all if the girls where sent back to Jamaica to complete their education. For one thing this would work out cheaper and they could stay with their grand mother and have the life away from the current situation being faced by the Wilkes family. The kids were taking care of Mia rather then the other way round, Mia would hardly get out of bed, food, and house keeping was usually down to Abigail. Dennard wondered if the kids were away from Mia, she would dust herself off and make the best of her current predicament. So early in 1961, the girls got shipped back to Jamaica and Dennard and Mia were left all alone in the house. Things did improve slightly, as Mia was forced to take up house chores; she made a concerted effort in getting used to the environment. The Wilkes made some friends, not in their street but in and around Brixton. The Caribbean community seemed to be increasing; there were community meetings, dances and indoor parties. To help Mia integrate into the community, Dennard made sure they attended as much social function as possible, mainly dances. The fun was not just attending the dance, but the entire preparation, the music and the feeling of belonging to a group of people irrespective of the goings on in the neighbourhood.

The dances were the single most important thing among the black community that gave them a sense of participating in the swinging sixties, a sense of belonging. At this stage of fashion, black was relegated to the background; the idea was to remove as much as possible of any semblance of "Black is beautiful", the Anglo-Saxon beauty lead the way to the detriment of black women where Afro-Caribbean lips, hips and hair were devalued. Women were forced to adapt more to the Anglo-Saxon beauty regime, in the form of coiffured hairdo, slender look, thin lips and faces covered in make-up. The black community took much joy in dressing up for the dances; women in horrock dresses, fully gathered skirt, the skirt was ideal for the high-energy Ska dance moves, the music of the time, and much favoured for its dignified elegance. Women alternated the formal look with a more casual style by wearing pastel coloured Capri pants, matching tie-tops, winkle picker shoes, white pop socks and pointy eye-glasses or sunglasses. It was a throwback to fifties Hollywood. Highly stylised grooming wasn't just the sole premise of women; men were expected to look their best as well, they also took the time out to refine their look. Men mostly wore sharp suits in dark colours, pork pie hats, white crisp pristine cotton shirts, narrow tapered trousers, which had to be a good three inches shorter than floor length, highly polished black Clarke-style shoes and fitted jackets, were often met with the sign of approval from the ladies. They looked elegant and felt good and when they congregated in the dance hall, it was a feeling of community, a place where they could be and act as "black" as they wanted without fear of reprisals or alienation. Dennard and Mia enjoyed dressing up and attending the dances, they met up with old friends and made new ones, the support and community network was getting better and life at home in Santly Street was a lot more bearable. Saying that though, more middleclass white families had moved out and two more black families had moved in. The working class white families were feeling pushed out which lead to a heightening of tensions between the two races in the street. Rather than the black families cowering in their homes, with the addition of more families, they were now being bold and going out, trying to claim their right to be in the neighbourhood which was bound to upset the original settlers. Dennard, like so many other black men at the time, discovered that for the right to live in the street, the right for his wife to walk down the street without fear of intimidation, he had to be aggressive, he had to develop an attitude, he was constantly on his guard, ready to defend or attack either by words or by physical intervention. This he noticed was now very common among the black community, every black man has had to physically defend himself or attack someone due to racial slurs or alienation from public buildings or at the place of work. Dennard's personal experience happened on his way home from work. His group of friends thought they had a foolproof system, but that wasn't the case. To eliminate or minimise the chances of being attacked or abused, most black people in those days avoided the public transport system, apart from the issue of attack, it was too expensive anyway and the money could be better used somewhere else. Black folk tended to walk miles to and from work, usually in groups as a form of protection. Usually, each group broke up as they each branched off to their individual streets, which through planning they made sure members of each group were living very close to each other. Dennard, as the last member of a five man group tended to walk the last five miles alone, which in itself wasn't bad, considering Dennard was a big strapping lad, with huge shoulders, over six feet in height and huge arms and hands. Others within the group believed he could take care of himself and anyone in their right mind wouldn't dare mess with him, black or white, or so you would think. It was a Thursday, late evening, same old British November weather, dark, muggy, with a slight hint of rain in the air, it was bitterly cold and there were little traces of the famous ever present London "smog". He had just left the last of the group, just by the Town hall and he was making his way gingerly home, tired from the day's proceedings, when he got accosted by three white men.

"Boy", they shouted, a derogatory term used in the old slave enclave of the deep south of America, where do you think you are going?

He tried to ignore them, as sometimes they get bored and leave you alone, but these lot were drunk, it was the weekend, they persisted and went on to stand in his path, shoving their red drunken faces in his, he knew there was only one way out of this situation, fight. He knew if he ran, they would chase and eventually catch him, worst still he could make it home and then that in itself would be the start of another nightmare, as they would take note of his house and derive much pleasure in coming back later at night to throw bricks through his windows or lay waiting for him whenever they had nothing else on for entertainment, no, flight was not an option. He studied the three men, tried to pick out the most vocal, hoped the other two were only partaking due to his egging them on, grabbed hold of him by the throat, Dennard was a big lad, he pulled the guy up to his head level, looking him straight in the eye as he choked and went from a red colour to a purplish bluish tint, the guys feet where dangling a couple of feet above the ground. By now the other two were trying to dislodge Dennard's grip to no avail, they tried punching him in the gut, pulled his arms and kicked him in the shins. Another trick picked up by black men at the time was the use of the Jamaican dialect, even though they could speak English without the dialect; it was observed that they were thought to be more sinister when the dialect is used. By this stage, the man with his throat being squeezed by Dennard was practically begging for his life, Dennard whispered in his face, taking his time, picking his words one at a time for clarity,

"If you wan live, you white trash, you better nat try a black man who jus come from Jamaica with weed in im lungs!"

Then he drops him on the pavement. The guy is on the pavement spluttering, trying to regain some air into his lungs, while his friends look up at Dennard with abject fear, they help their friend up and scupper, Dennard, scared out of his wits for what could have happened, puts on an aggressive look, just in case anyone else in the vicinity wanted to take up the challenge.

By 1965, the neighbourhood in Brixton had taken on a different look compared to the one the Wilkes came across in the early sixties. The Wilkes had moved up in the world through hard graft, their current landlord was selling up and moving on, apparently he was unhappy with the type of clientele in Brixton. Luckily, he made it known and Dennard, after discussing with Mia of course, decided to buy it off him. The landlord and the rest of the neighbourhood wondered where black people found the huge deposit required for buying a house. The trick was that all Caribbean's at this stage contributed a monthly sum to a pot within a group of five to six people and each member of the group took it in turns to pick up the pot. Dennard had previously picked two pots and the money was sitting in the house unused, he was actually thinking of sending some to Jamaica. The Wilkes had planned to convert the property back into a five-bedroom family home once the tenancy agreement of the last tenant to move out was completed. It took the Wilkes three months to get rid of all the tenants and another six months to complete the conversion into a family home. There were a lot more Caribbean families, Africans and Asians, the culture, though still mainly white, were taking on a black tinge with the remaining white folks accepting their new neighbours. Dennard and Mia were just coming round to the idea of bringing the girls back to England when the unexpected happened, Mia got pregnant. The dances, social function and the more relaxed feel of the neighbourhood had given Mia a new lease of life, Dennard had noticed how she pounced on him with Gusto after their visit to dances, which were viewed as a form of foreplay anyway. Early in 1966, they had a healthy baby boy, Dave Wilkes. The Wilkes had by now agreed that it may be advantageous for the girls to remain in Jamaica, at least up until their school certificate, they could then come to England for their university education, they thought coping with Dave would be such a hassle that the idea of having three teenage girls around at the same time could send Mia over the edge yet again. A decision that would haunt them as it would greatly affect the relationship between them and the girls and that of Dave and the girls, but hey, for now, it was the best or only option they had.

CHAPTER 6

It was going on half past nine, the atmosphere at parks wine bar was taking on a new look again due to the level of people present and the type of music. The wine bar had a very distinct look and feel, as you come into parks; there is an alcove with club lights above, with wooden floors, the only part of Parks with wooden floors. This area prior to now would usually have two set of chairs, set up in restaurant style rather than the living room feel of the rest of the bar, the chairs and table are easily movable and so are the lights. A few people, wanting to sit up in restaurant fashion would sit at these tables for their meals prior to retiring to the easy chairs for drinks and cigarettes. At nine pm exactly, these chairs and tables would miraculously disappear and a little dance floor revealed. The music usually stays the same, slow, cool with nothing frenzied. A major difference between Parks and other wine bars is the fact that the DJs they employ must be mute; they do not utter a word, its just one long continuous music throughout the night. None of the usual DJ crap utterances we are used to like "shout out to my gal who is 30 or 20 years old today", no! This is uninterrupted, undiluted pure music. The usual thing is for a maximum of three to four couples slow dancing on the dance floor, nothing sleazy, just intense lovers grooving to the music, without a care in the world, actually the world is usually not present at that time to the dancers anyway. They are usually in a world of their own. The dress code is usually smart casual, which means no jeans, face caps, hoods or sneakers. Chav's were turned away at the door.

By this time we had shifted around the table a bit, I was now sitting close to the lamp with Abe beside me on the easy chair, Baz and Dave sat on the chair facing us, with Dave closer to me looking a bit tipsy, legs on the central table, arms splayed alongside the easy chair,

Hey, do you want me to order some coffee? I ask Dave, I need you firing on all cylinders tonight, I have issues needing resolution, so don't think of going all drunk on me.

He ignores me, leans towards the central table for his drink, takes a huge swig of his beer and directs a huge belch in my direction,

Look, just because you have issues doesn't mean the rest of us have to sit here and be miserable, I am out to have fun, if I want to be miserable, I would spend time with my family and in answer to your question, no, I do not want coffee.

That's a terrible thing to say, you mean you are miserable when you are with your parents, ask Abe?

No! You plunker, I meant my sisters, cousins and extended family, countered Dave. Well, I for one enjoy the company of my siblings, saying that though, I've only got the one brother.

Well good for you, May I assume you guys grew up together in the same house with your parents?

Well, yes, didn't you?

No, answered Dave, which as far as I can see is the cause of most of the issues in my family.

You have a point there you know, absent parents.

Don't even start on that, says Baz, I can see where you are heading, the issue of black men not being parents to their kids which then leads to unruly kids, bad society and so on, what has that got to do with being black British?

A lot in my book, my upbringing included several beatings by my dad, parents in this current England aren't allowed to sneeze on their kids, they are whisked away to jail for child abuse. Apart from the Government interfering in child upbringing, they also provide money to the mothers thereby nullifying the authority of the black male, mothers, who now have choices are fast to kick fathers out of the house and claim benefit. The funny thing is that the same mothers, usually black females now claim that there are not enough good black men around and the few that there are, are being snapped up by white women.

Baz, looks at me all confused, so, I'll repeat the question, what the hell has that got to do with being black British.

Jeez, someone help me out here, I'm lost for words, Abe, what do you think?

Well, look at the bigger picture, black British includes both males and females, right? But the soul of a community are made up of the males, the males are the gels holding the family together, now, if the males have lost their identity or their roles and responsibilities within the society, then how will they be in a position to direct the so called weaker sex? The idea being, the more you downgrade the black male, the less there is structure in the black community and the less people are able to understand what black British stands for. Does that explain your thinking, Ade? Asked Abe

I nod vigorously in answer to his question; making a sweeping like motion with my hands implying to everyone the fact that Abe was spot on.

Hold on a minute, this same Government rules applies to the white males as well, how is that they have no problem with their identity? Baz Said.

Dave, suddenly wakes up from his far away thoughts and launches into a tirade, as you know, we are trying to understand blacks, these are a race who have come from differing cultural backgrounds to that of whites, the cultural differences is most obvious especially when you compare Africans to the whites, as said earlier, the relationship between a black African male and his son to that of a white male with his son are different, the whites have been used to that sort of relationship, but with a black British man of African origin or Caribbean origin, he is having to refocus his thinking, having to be all touchy feely, just to fit the Governments agenda. This will mess with his head, so apart from the black man trying to realign himself to the new Mr nice guy, you are also expecting him to redefine himself as British in a place where he doesn't really feel British and he hasn't been made to feel British.

So the question is, how do you make him feel British, asked Abe?

Well, stop messing with his head for a start, shouts Dave!

Seriously though, in the good old days, the black male knew exactly his position in society or within the family, now those lines are blurred.

Okay, lets examine the American situation, I jumped in, the blacks from America, who I might add were taken there as slaves, got their freedom prior to being recognised as Americans. Apart from the prior mentioned issues, they now had the misfortune of having to endure years of segregation and humiliation, and still today they surfer racial hatred but in spite of all these barriers, a Black American is extremely proud to stand and be counted as an American, why?

Now, superimpose that unto the Black British, we were not brought to England as slaves, we did not work in any cotton fields, there was segregation but not as bad as it was in America, so why are we so reluctant to stand up proud and state our allegiance to the queen?

Ah, shouts Abe, you have hit the nail on the head right there, the Americans and the queen.

Huh! We look at Abe all confused

What the hell are you on about, said Baz?

Well, just think about it, Americans do not really have a place they can call home apart from America, that's why some of them are trying desperately to trace their roots to African countries, while we British blacks do not have that problem, we can categorically say where we are from, be it the Caribbean or Africa. Due to this main difference, we always refer to our country of origin as "home", unknowingly categorising England as a thoroughfare, somewhere or someplace for us to make a living and then move on. Ninety percent of black British when asked where they'll retire would say categorically their country of origin; this is not the case for Americans. Now the issue of the queen, the Americans salute God, country and the dollar, that's an easy pill to swallow, to pledge allegiance just to the queen, especially when you think of all the atrocities committed by men all in the name of the queen is sometimes a little too hard to swallow.

We must have all sat there staring at Abe for a good five minutes with blank looks on our faces,

Where is that waiter, shouts Dave, I was close to getting drunk a minute ago, what happened to remove that nice feeling.

Abe happened, says Baz!

You guys, I don't understand, do you think that analogy is incorrect? It explains totally why we are different from the Americans and why we seem unable to agree or accept the tag black British, it definitely explains why there are more home grown terrorist in England compared to the United States. If these issues weren't there, I am sure, just like the Americans, we'll be completely happy to stand on our high horse shouting at everyone who cares to listen, I'm a black British citizen.

Thinking about it, Abe could be right on some level, but it isn't that simple, I add, there are several other issues preventing blacks accepting the tag black British, one issue which seems to rear its ugly head during football matches involving England is this issues of being British or English. The English use the term British in a derogatory way. You are either English or you are Irish, welsh or Scottish, which to the English is the same as using the dreaded nigger word! But they dare not mention that in public, but they can make jokes about Scottish people in public, that's acceptable.

Every time I hear those jokes about not being English and the way others cope with it, it just makes me more determined to remind my kids, when I eventually have them, that they are and would always be black African's first and then British second.

But saying that though, the welsh and Scots don't care about being English, in fact to them its more like a bad thing, said Baz.

Which is fine, I answer but look at it another way, if the English are racial towards the Scots and the welsh to the point they had to create a different entity just as wrapper for the three sections of England, then what hope do the black British have in being integrated into a group of people who are less than integrated. If the Welsh, Scots and Irish are not so keen on accepting the tag Scot, Welsh or Irish British then why the hell should the black community of England be so keen to want to take on black British?

Finally the drinks arrive; we are left in our own thoughts again for about five minutes as we each take a swig of our drinks, no one really keen to carry on the discussion. Dave makes to get up, staggers a bit towards me, I rush to catch him before he tumbles over.

I will not be responsible for you tonight, could someone get that beer away from him and order some coffee, I said, to no one in particular, I'll be taking this fool to the toilets, now, I hope by the time we get back there is coffee on that table for Dave rather than a beer.

Abe looks on anxiously, will you be okay with him, he asks? Well, if he is about to fall and I find myself falling with him, note that I will be leaving him to hit the deck by his lonesome self, don't fancy sharing that bit of the fun. I practically have to carry Dave to the loo; he is barely able to walk in a straight line. As we get to the loos, I'm thinking, at least if he falls down flat on his face here, there'll be little chance of him catching anything from the floors. The toilets here are as posh as they come, hot towels, expensive hand wash on the sinks, creams and an attendant present. There were ten cubicles, all self contained, the floors were marble with the wash hand basins and loos fitted with gold taps and handles. The smell was the thing that really got you, it wasn't a typical toilet smell, no, this was very different, it smelled more like the perfume section of a huge store like marks and Spencer or Harrods or something and it was very weird. As we make our way into the toilet, I leave Dave to make his way to a cubicle while I attempted to go into a another, Dave looks at me all apologetic, pleading with eyes for me to help him in, I say to myself, one more shove in the right direction wouldn't kill me, so I did. Then he gets in to his cubicle and gives me another look, forget it mate, don't even think about it, if you can't do your own trousers and handle your instrument, then you might as well do it in your bloody pants.

See ya!

I leave him standing there looking foolish. I finish my business and wait for Dave by the door, hoping he wasn't drowning in the toilet bowl, anyway; luckily he walks out heading straight for the door without pausing to acknowledge me,

Hold on a minute, I says, didn't we come in here together?

Well, we don't have to leave together, Dave answered.

I hope you weren't expecting me to hold your little willy while you peed?

We somehow get to our table without any one falling over, and there on the table was a hot cup of coffee waiting for Dave, nice! That should wake him up, he needs to have all his faculties around him and also I didn't fancy the idea of having to drive him home. We sit down and the rest of us watch as Dave sips his coffee, its usually the same thing, he'll have a sip, splutter and spit it out complaining about the taste spoiling his beer tongue, so we sit there waiting for the inevitable which never came. It seems Dave was looking to be sober tonight for a change, he must be getting into the discussion and this would be a first for him, not spitting out the coffee.

Why is it that we do not bring our women here, I'll quite like to be slow dancing with my lady right this minute, says Abe, if I had one.

It wasn't a rule written in blood, it just happened that this is the guys night out, a night where the women understood as gospel that the men where going out to hunt and that was that, no argument or discussion about it. It's about us men, as the head and hopefully providers taking control of something in our lives rather than just following the latest trend as set by either the Government or our live in ladies.

On saying that though, there is nothing stopping you picking up a bird and having a bit of a slow dance, we won't tell if you don't.

Baz looked around the bar, as far as I can tell; the folks who come here are usually attached, so there are couples everywhere without a single unattached female insight. Your dancing partner doesn't necessarily have to be female, you can pick any of the males present, suggests Dave,

Are you offering, retorts Baz?

Guys, Abe jumps in, aren't we going off course here? I personally think our experiences growing up in England could have contributed to our inability to accept the tag of black British.

Oh for the love of Christ, give it a rest mate, you are giving me a bloody headache, moans Dave; please pick another topic for conversation.

Nah man! Can anyone remember his nursery or primary school experience?

Mine wasn't that great, said Abe

CHAPTER 7

Birmingham 1970

Kwame and Esi Abrefo came to England in 1966; they left Ghana just as the then prime minister, Nkrumah was fast changing from an elected prime minister to a dictator. The prime minister had recently changed the country into a one-party state. Just as they made it to England, the Ghanaian army overthrew Nkrumah's regime. Abebe was just three years old. On their arrival in Britain, they headed straight for Birmingham, where Kwame's cousin, Kofi, lived. In the years following World War II there was a major influx of British Commonwealth country immigrants into Birmingham, with large communities from Asia and the Caribbean's settling in the city. In the post war years, a massive program of slum clearances took place, and vast areas of the city were re-built, with overcrowded "back to back" housing being replaced by high-rise blocks of flats. The city centre was also extensively re-built, especially the Bull Ring Shopping Centre. Birmingham also became a centre of the national motorway network. A new Central Reference Library was completed in the 1970s, and the nearby area around Broad Street, including the canal network, Centenary Square, the ICC and Brindleyplace, was extensively renovated, Kofi's one bed flat was on Broad Street in one of the high-rise blocks. The living conditions weren't great but at least it was a roof over their heads. Kofi though was single, had a live-in girl friend in his apartment. The Abrefo family had to make do with the living room for their accommodation arrangements. Abe probably spent all of a month to two at the apartment prior to being sent off to a nanny's place and then onto nursery where he spent the next ten years, of course he came home for the occasional weekends and school holidays but that was the sum total of the time spent living with his parents. Kwame and Esi worked hard, played less and had little time for anything else. Kwame had three brothers, two sisters and several extended family members back in Accra depending on him for not just their livelihood but also education for their kids as well. Esi also had three siblings dependent on her for sustenance. The

Abrefo's also had the added complication of having to study to achieve an education. Kofi on the other hand was from a wealthy family in Ghana, he came to England on holiday and decided to stay rather than go back to Ghana to take over his father's business as earmarked for him. Suffice to say, his dad, after several unsuccessful years of trying to convince him to come back home had finally resorted to the drastic means of disowning him and cutting him off from the family wealth. This did not deter Kofi, but it did seriously affect his living standard. He was striving very hard to get used to the idea of working, earning money and paying bills, but it was proving to be harder than he expected. The Abrefo's dropped in on Kofi just as he was fast running out of money and jobs, they became his meal ticket, he took them in on the understanding that they had to help out with the bills, what he failed to explain to the Abrefo's was that rather than helping out with the bills, they were actually paying the bills, providing food and generally in charge of anything in the household involving money. It was a very tough time for The Abrefo's.

Abe's early years were spent in Hansworth, not something he likes to linger on; he could remember the jokes the giggles and the idiotic questions from fellow children on the playground. The sort of questions asked by well meaning curious kids, seeing a black person for the first time,

"Why are you called coloured, you have brown skin?

Why do you have brown lines on your hands?

Why does your hair look so funny?

Why, why, why, it was never ending and when he did open his mouth to answer, they all laughed at his accent. Abe learned to keep his mouth shut for the next couple of years while he studied the way the other kids talked. It was thought he was shy, which he wasn't, he just didn't fancy the taunts whenever he opened his gob to say something. He remembers sitting in the playground all by himself, studying the other kids as they played, straining with every muscle in his body, listening to the kids talk, trying to pick the nuances and gestures. He stared so intently at the other kids, they labelled him Mr creepy. In the privacy of his bedroom late at night, he would practice talking with a British accent; he would practice making the same gestures as the other kids did. He promised himself to never place himself in a position where he is laughed at due to his spoken English. There was one girl at the nursery that took a shine to him, Nancy O'Connor. That's one name he will always remember, sometimes-fond memories; other times with the fear he felt then when she decided to make him her personal project. Abe didn't quite understand why Nancy was teased by the other kids, just like he was, for one thing she was white just like they were, but towards the end of his time at the institution, he found out she was an Irish girl, like that explained it all, he still didn't have a clue why she was a target. Rumour had it she came from London, via Dublin, her parents worked in London, and mum was a prostitute while dad was into the gangland lifestyle. Another version was that her parents were a young couple looking to break into the show business world of music, Nancy never gave any impression of the real version of truth, when asked about her parents, she was always vague and most times just dismissive. The point was that she felt a kinship towards Abe and went out of her way to make friends, well, that's the way she probably saw it. Abe's recollection of their first encounter was at the dinning table, Nancy, compared to the other kids, was a big tall girl, even at a young tender age of just five, she had long jet black hair, her skin was pale, very pale compared to others, thought Abe, everything about her face looked pointed, chin, nose, forehead, even her head. She had big very dark grey eyes, which looked even bigger in her face due to her pale look; she had a way of putting the frighteners on you by just one sideways glance. Abe remembers her coming over to him at the dinning table, sits down, sneering,

What are you looking at?

Abe, being Abe, shuffles over giving her room without a word. Abe rushes his dinner, gets up and leaves the room, Nancy promptly follows, tugs his shirt, you know something, you are bit all right, you are not like the others,

Duh! You think, replies Abe,

She ignores the remark and carries on without acknowledging the interruption. Well, apart from the fact that you are black, they seem to hate you more than they hate me anyway. I'll talk to you later, and like that Abe and Nancy became best buddies. She would always seek him out; invite him to join her on some run, walk or play. At first Abe was very reluctant, wanting to keep his own company, and actually not sure who he should be more scared off, the others teasing him or Nancy wanting to be his friend, he was at a dilemma as to why she would want to be friends with him in the first place. Nancy kept on the chase, genuine reluctance on Abe's part soon turned to excitement but he kept up the pretence of being forced, also the idea that he was being forced seemed to give Nancy some sort of joy.

The years went by and Abe found life that little bit more bearable the longer he stayed there, the other kids soon got used to him and they treated him more as the rest, some of the other kids were soon jealous of his special friendship with Nancy and wondered why they spent so much time together. Life at the nursery carried on with the mundane things, like growing up learning and just keeping busy and staying alive. The monotony was broken by the odd weekend visit to his parents, or Kofi's visits to the nursery. Kofi's visits to his nursery left him concerned and confused, it sometimes felt like he was there just to tick some imaginary boxes. Visit times at the nursery adhered to a strict timetable, Kofi came in five to ten minutes just before the end of visitation time, he was very clinical in his approach and he would examine Abe, make sure there were no visible scars, no broken bones and no loss of weight or teeth. He would ask all the usual questions, like, was he okay, did he sleep enough, ate enough or played with the other kids, he seemed to take notes. The other strange thing he couldn't understand was the fact that Kofi seemed to have a different girl on his arm anytime he visited, his girls were always white. Abe found out later as an adult that Kofi had been paid by his parents to visit, confirm he was okay and then report back. On one of his several visit homes, he overheard his dad having a conversation with Kofi about his penchant for going out with white girls despite the inherent dangers that particular course of action posed to him. Kofi's explanation was simple yet complicated, his first issue was that he wasn't ready to be married; his second issue was that he couldn't afford to take any black girl out due to the fact that life with them often ends up being too expensive for him. Apparently, going out with a white girl was simple, they didn't ask for much, they were quite happy to sit at home and watch telly or go down the road to the local pub, and when do they do go out, they were always willing to pick up their share of the tab. On the other hand, the black girls were usually not interested in staying indoors, especially if they had spent so much money on their hair, cloths, shoes and bags, they wanted to go to the most expensive club or wine bar, they were also never keen to pay their share, in fact they considered it an insult to their womanhood if the man didn't pick up all the expense of the night out. Kofi's current financial situation didn't make for a good relationship with a black girl, his third and final issue was that white girls looked up to him and his sexual prowess, even if he was crap at it, they seemed to have a curious bone itching, desperately needing a scratch, whereas the black girls were unwilling to put out until they had a marriage proposal on the table. Anyway, Kofi's current philosophy was to snag them white, shag them white and marry them black, if and when you can afford it. Abe gave up trying to understand Kofi. Abe's next major life changing event happened at around age eight to nine, he couldn't exactly remember when but it was something he would always remember fondly. It was one of those evenings, as always, there were few nursery school attendants looking after the kids at dinner time, the one male attendant was drunk, asleep in one of the many closets, thinking no one knew, whereas it was common knowledge, while the female attendant was off somewhere in the building yakking on the phone. The kids were all just sitting down to dinner, all ten or so of them, everyone trying to get a comfortable sit and just the right set of starter, main course and pudding. It was one of those very miserable nights, it had been raining for some time, it was cold and there was the occasional lightening. The old house shook violently from the howling wind; you could hear the tree branches banging against the windowpanes outside as well as the rain. The building was located in a very deserted area; the nearest building was a couple of miles out. The noise of the rain, lighting and the branches was just about being drowned out by the noise of the children eating when suddenly the lights went out. There was pandemonium as kids started screaming, running in all directions, not knowing where they were headed. Kids crashed into tables, food got hurled high in the air, drinks got sprayed, which all added to the panic. Abe was able to call on his experience of growing up in Accra where the occasional lack of electricity was common place, this lead to a keen sense of direction and an ability to navigate in the dark, as it was common place for the electricity to be suddenly turned off. Abe grabbed hold of Nancy, who was sat next to him when the lights went out; they headed to the nearest closet, closed the door and huddled together. Abe couldn't remember exactly how long they were in there, but he did remember Nancy holding on very tightly to his hand with her left hand, he remembered her slowly moving her right hand up and down his arm, this went on for at least five to ten minutes, Abe was frightened and excited at the same time, not really sure why. The closet that once felt like a safe heaven from the chaotic scenes outside now felt a lot more dangerous. Nancy seemed to be trembling; Abe instinctively felt a rush of protective feelings towards her. All of a sudden, the closet took on a different feel, Abe suddenly felt himself floating on air, rather than the oppressive pitch black darkness, Abe felt a cool breeze, it was as if they were sat under the stars at the top of some scenic mountain, just the two of them alone in the world holding hands. He reached round her shoulders to pull her closer; he felt her thin cotton blouse, which was wet from some of the spilled drink during the mad rush in the dinning. Nancy sank her head into his chest, while he stroked her hair, he didn't quite know why he was doing that, but it seemed to do the trick as her trembling subsided, she looked up into his eyes after a couple of minutes, he could just about make out her smile and wide eyes,

She asked, do you feel like a wee?

Yes, answered Abe,

That means you like me, replied Nancy,

No I don't! Abe protested, shoving her away from him, just as the closet door flew open, brightness shinning into the closet, a voice shouted over the din,

Found another two in here!

Abe avoided Nancy for the next couple of months following the closet incident, but he always caught himself seeking her out with his eyes, which was reciprocal because he caught her looking at him as well. Life at home had changed somewhat; Kwame and Esi were doing a lot better than Kofi and they now had their own place on Broad Street, which meant Kofi had to get a job to pay his rent and bills. The Abrefo's still had crazy hours at work and college but at least Abe had his own room when he came home on holiday and the occasional weekend. He spent those few days stuck in doors all alone with the television or an occasional visit from a starving Kofi who came in like a tornado, devouring every edible thing in his path. He barely had time to say hello to Abe on his way in and out of the flat with a pit stop at the kitchen, a quick tank fill up and tara, see you later, say hello to your parents and he was gone like the wind, Abe left wondering if that was a dream or his imagination playing tricks on him. His parents on the odd occasions when they were at home over the weekends, had friends over, they would play west African high life music, drink and talk all day about the different West African countries and their issues, it was civil war here, military coup there or democratic elections here. It always struck Abe as odd, how British politics was never discussed but football was discussed just never British politics or issues affecting blacks in England. It seemed to his parents, they were in England only for a short time; they will be going back to Ghana as soon as it was humanly possible and therefore there was no reason to get involved in the local politics or issues affecting blacks in the community. Abe felt that he had a separate agenda to that of his parents, where he was trying his best to integrate and be as British as he could, his parents seemed to be sticking their heads in the sand by constantly reminding themselves of home and keeping faith with everything to do with home. It became increasingly difficult to communicate with his parents as the only topics of conversation they were interested in had to do with his studies or Ghana, they would not entertain the idea of any typical English social event. Abe soon figured out how to get his parents signature on his field trip forms without having to explain to them the educational value to him visiting a museum, a dairy farm and so on. It was cousin Kofi to the rescue, of course at a price, which he duly collected without so much as a backward glance. The older Abe got, the less inclined he felt towards coming home on weekends or holidays, preferring to spend the time at school. Just as things were looking comfortable financially for the Abrefo's, Esi got pregnant, apparently unplanned, still it didn't do much for Abe and his relationship with his parents. He felt a lot happier when he was at school playing or talking with Nancy, who he eventually patched things up with.

Abe and Nancy got over their initial embarrassment about finding out they both liked each other after a couple of months and things more or less got back to normal with their friendship. The only difference now was that they were both sometimes slightly uncomfortable during certain instances, like Abe mistakenly brushing against her chest or mistakenly brushing against each others arm, this was in spite of the fact that they were both going out of their way to make sure it happened.

Unknowingly to Abe, this was his first true love, the one person he felt he could and wanted to spend time with, the one person he would seek out whenever they were at the playground, either physically or just by a quick glance around the playground. Nancy had been in the nursery at least six to eight years before her parents came for the solitary visit which more or less put paid to her continued stay at the nursery. It was a day Abe would always remember. There were mid week visitation and weekend visitation, most parents preferred to visit during the weekend. It was a beautiful summer's day, with parents camping out in the big garden. Days like these, the nursery do put in an effort in making parents feel welcome, they present the look and feel of a family environment. The garden was in great shape, lawn trimmed, balloons floating from the roof, swings cleaned and mended, fence painted, broken garden gate mended and it was generally a happy place. Kids were genuinely happy, it was infectious really and you couldn't help but feel happy, even if you didn't have any visitors. On days like these, kids who usually don't have visitors hang around the garden hoping for crumbs from other parents who take pity on them, all kids are made to dress up, look their best, when you spot your visitor, you ran to meet them with a great big grin on your face, there will be no crying, moaning or complaining to parents or else. Anyways, Nancy and Abe usually end up on the staircase leading to the kitchen, sat there admiring the other kids playing with either their siblings or their parents, being pampered by their parents. They would sit there all day, holding hands and having a giggle; Abe remembered when they shared their first kiss on that staircase. It was a typical visitation day; Abe and Nancy were left on the staircase all day and it got late and dark. Nancy got cold, so Abe cuddled her, just to keep her warm, nothing else, just before they went in, when all the visitors had finally left, Nancy took one last look at the garden, gazed up into the sky, squeezed Abe's hand and said she would rather have this time with Abe than with her parents, she then leaned forward and kissed Abe. Abe knew he liked Nancy, how much he wasn't quite sure but now he was in love, and their love was sealed by the kiss. In all their time at the nursery, Abe had about three visits from his parents and about half a dozen or so from Kofi, usually; Abe would invite Nancy round to talk to his parents or Kofi anytime they visited. Abe's parents were not cold or anything towards her but they were not overly friendly, on the other hand Kofi was usually extremely friendly, introducing her to whoever his latest girlfriend was while referring to Nancy as Abe's girlfriend, which made both of them all shy and tongue tied. On this faithful day in 1975, her parents popped in on their way to a gig, so we found out later. As per usual, Nancy and I were sat on the staircase resigned to our faith of being left out of all the fun when suddenly Nancy is called to the administration room. After a couple of minutes, she comes out into the garden with a very tall, blond, slender looking woman, she looked like an angel and she was just as beautiful. The dad couldn't be bothered to leave the comfort of his car. Everyone stared at her as she walked towards a secluded part of the garden, then suddenly a parent shouted,

Aren't you the singer, straining, desperate to remember her name, I love your songs, Nancy's mum didn't break stride, she just kept on walking towards the chairs and table. By that single act, everyone got the message, so she was left alone. Abe sat on the staircase for another couple of hours, watching Nancy and her mum, wondering, she should have called me over to meet her mum, but it never happened. Nancy and her mum then stood up, it seemed she was ready to leave, they walked towards Abe, the mum stopped, looked at Abe and then said something about not wanting Nancy to play with Abe anymore, she had heard rumours that they were best of friends. She said something about not wanting her baby girl becoming a black person, as if it was catching and she didn't understand why we were allowed in the nursery, no one told her about blacks being allowed in this nursery, she shrieked.

All I could remember was the eerie silence that fell on the garden, it was a slow motion film, Abe could see Nancy by her mum, held tightly, tears streaking down her pale pinched face, she had a look in her eye, Abe, couldn't figure it out, was it a look of pity or fear? The other parents looked away, embarrassed but not saying anything, it felt like an eternity before the head teacher came out into the garden, held Abe's hand, pulling him close to her before chastising Nancy's mum, fingers wagging, head shaking vigorously,

Everyone is welcomed here, Mrs O'Connor, please go into the office.

That was the last time Abe saw Nancy O'Connor as a kid.

CHAPTER 8

We had gone through another round of musical chairs at parks wine bar, I was now sat near Baz with Dave and Abe sat close together. Apart from a few regulars and some die hard drinkers, the wine bar was fast emptying out, it was nicely quiet, well, quiet as can be with music blaring out of some huge speakers strategically placed around the bar. You could now have a conversation without the need for shouting to be heard above the hubbub of the bar or having to move extremely close to whomever you were having the conversation. I wasn't that impressed with Abe's childhood stories. Having a childhood in England, Africa or India, shouldn't really determine your adulthood, as an adult you can make your own choices,

I disagree, says Dave and that's mainly why there is so much hostility between you Africans and the

British born blacks or the Caribbean's. You are unable to understand or accept the deep psychological scar inflicted on those of us not lucky enough to grow up in a place where you are the first class citizen rather than the second-class citizen we are forced to endure.

Cobblers, shouts Baz, whatever racial segregation or racial humiliation suffered in England, those of us who had the advantage of growing up away from racial turmoil had other issues to contend with, like caste, tribalism, class segregation and so on. But that most have been less painful, to be relegated just because you are darker than your fellow countrymen can't be as hurtful as being relegated due to the fact that you were none white, answers Dave.

Oh well, I guess you are only able to relate to your own personal circumstances and experiences, says me, but my argument is that you should get to a point in your life where you delineate yourself from your childhood issues and stand as an adult, accept your lot in life and make the best use of the situation. If we constantly refer back to issues that happened to us in our childhood, it would always hold us back, it's like an open wound; it will refuse to heal the more you keep picking at it. Don't get me wrong, I am not saying that your childhood experiences should not shape who you are today but in the same vein it shouldn't hold you back. The main difference between African British and the Caribbean British is that the African's accept their lot in life; come over to England with the sole purpose of making a better life for themselves, no matter what it takes. This could obviously sometimes lead to illegal actions as they are usually so desperate to succeed, but the idea is to ignore the nastiness around you and achieve a better life for yourself despite the unfairness of the world you are in. Wow! That's a lot of assumption, said Dave, you are assuming that the Caribbean's are not willing to make something of themselves or that they are so wrapped up in their past, they are unable to move forward.

Okay, explain to me why there are several Asian millionaires and not so many millionaires of Caribbean Descent? I ask,

Baz jumps into the conversation, I don't think that has anything to do with childhood issues, as far as Asians are concerned, they are driven to achieve the most financially wherever they are Asia, Africa or England and it doesn't really matter, Asians are like Jews in that respect.

Well, my sentiments exactly, says me, I do concede that childhood experiences make you into the adult you are today but it should work both ways, it should either spur you on to greatness or cripple you to a non existence, its your choice.

The choices you make are what makes you guys go into criminal activities, said Dave. Which guys, asks Abe?

Asians and Africans, answered Dave.

To answer your initial question, the same could be said of Africans, apart from the dictators who have siphoned money away from starving children in their respective countries, there are not that many British millionaires of African Descent, It so infuriating when everyone assumes any criminal activity must be down to us "Yardies", police stop and search is mostly directed at us, house raids car checks. Nah man! That's not just a black Caribbean thing, shouts Abe, police harassment is the prerogative of all ethnic minorities.

Well, saying that though, there was a time when police had a lot more on their plate, the IRA era, that was one time it was safe to be black in London, the idea being, there were no black Irish IRA terrorist, said Dave.

That was the only time when as a black man you could drive around London, safe in the knowledge of not being pulled over by the police, it was definitely a peaceful time for us, wasn't it?

But that is not strictly true though, the idea that there are no Irish black men or is it? Ask Baz,

I'm sure there are, but the question was, were there any black IRA men, the answer was, not a chance. Black men do not fight over religion, we may fight over finance, drugs or women but never religion, answered Dave.

That may be true of black British men, but not of African or Asian men, there were lots of religious wars fought in Africa, between Muslims and Christians, added Abe. Yea, but that is understandable, what's completely unthinkable is Africans killing each other over the different sects within Christianity, I answered.

There may have been war between the different religion but sectarianism has never been an issue in Africa and neither is it an issue with British Africans and we can definitely without a shadow of doubt agree that black Caribbean British are not that religious to want to blow anything up. So ultimately, there were no IRA black men, thus no stopping or searching British black men for hidden bombs.

On saying that though, that situation lasted all of a couple of years, now the current al qaeda fundamentalist is a different ball game entirely, said Baz.

No! Abe said, its still the same thing, there are more Asian Muslims than there are black Muslims, so in theory, when the police go looking for fundamentalist rather than terrorist, they hopefully should leave black

British men alone, the same can't be said of Asians though!

What are you saying? An agitated Baz retorts! That all Asians are Muslim fundamentalist terrorist?

Nope! I didn't say that, you did, alls I am saying is that Muslim fundamentalist are either mostly Asians or Arabs, answered Abe, very rarely would you come across black African Muslim fundamentalist.

That's a load of hog wash, says me, the London bombings of 2005 had both Asians and black British men identified, so that blows holes in your argument.

No it doesn't, the few black British men identified were those who had lost their way, you couldn't really call them black men, said Abe.

Huh! Dave said, mirroring the rest of us.

Okay, let me explain, says Abe, there are some British black men who have lost their way and can't really take on the term black anymore, they are or should be called "uncle tom's". Their typical characteristics include; married to a white woman refuses to relate to their African or Caribbean roots, goes skiing, swimming and plays lawn tennis and the list goes on.

Hey! Hold on a minute; are you inferring that a typical black British man does not go skiing or swimming? Asked Baz,

Well, let me put it this way, Abe responds, as black men we like to look good, whatever we do, take for example athletics in Olympics, when those guys line up to run a hundred metres, have you noticed how the black guys are always the best dressed even in their running gear, they have chains round their necks, the females have chains on their ankles, the guys have gold plated running shoes, my point is, any sport where a black man is not good at, where he can not look good, he will not participate. Black British men are bad at swimming because when they go to the leisure centre as kids, they were too busy checking the babes out to concentrate on the swimming lessons and the females will not risk destroying their hairdo just for a poxy swim. In the case of skiing, any sport that is detrimental to the health, is a no go area for black men generally, this is why you wouldn't catch a black man doing things like bungee jumping, mountain climbing, sky diving and so on. The thinking behind this is if it is not a profitable venture, no point taking part in it. Now to return to the initial assertion, any black man taking part in the aforementioned activities has lost his way. Jeeze you are so full of crap, says Dave, I know loads of black guys who are good swimmers and who go skiing, and they have not lost their way as black men to my knowledge. Anyways, to return to the initial issue, those black men who took part in the London bombings of 2005 had been brainwashed into thinking they were something else, probably they were promised riches beyond their wildest dream, that's my thinking anyway, as far as I am aware, the only motivation for black men is money.

Don't be so cynical, I said, there a loads of black men out there, British, who are motivated by justice and fairness, peace, religion and so on, not every black British, either African or Caribbean, are motivated strictly by money.

You are making so many assumptions without there being someone here to defend the issues raised, interjected Dave, I might go as far as saying you may actually be exhibiting racist tendencies, except if your argument is based on the fact that you have recently married a white girl without informing any of us and you are talking from personal experience.

Dave was thinking of his sister, who, married to a nice white guy called Gary Chase, seems to be happy, as far as he was aware anyway. Take for example, your suggestion that black men, and may I assume when you use the word "men" it's in the biblical term? So this includes women as well, anyway, your assertion that those married to white women or men have lost their way, why and how did you come up with that, have you had any personal experience with a mixed race couple?

Abe took his time to answer, pausing to lean forward, pick up his drink and then slowly sipping it while the rest of us waited expectantly, looking at him for an answer, thinking he had argued himself into a corner without proof to back up his argument.

Abe leans forward to put his drink back on the table, signals to the waiter for another round of drinks as he leaned backwards. While the others stared at him intently, he was buying time, thinking of a good response.

Okay, could someone explain this to me? Answers Abe, finally, just as Dave was about to explode, does anyone round the table know of a black man married to a white woman who takes his wife to all their African or Caribbean family functions or to their local Afro-Caribbean restaurant with the guys or just generally hanging out with their black British friends, now let me be clear, I am not talking about their mutual friends, I am talking about hanging out with family, people the white wife or husband knew only after marriage or when they started going out?

Little did any one realise that Abe was going through his own personal turmoil. Dave was really getting wound up; he felt Abe was basing his arguments on hearsay or rumours without personally experiencing any of his assertions, this has always been the case with black British of African background, they made up their minds without trying to understand blacks of Caribbean background. Thinking of his sister, Ayana and her husband Gary, they did mix socially with the family and they did attend social functions with friends but the more he though about it, the more he had furrowed brows, he seemed to recall there being shift in his relationship with Ayana just after she started seeing Gary, he couldn't quite put his finger on why. His relationship with his three sisters was always fraught with issues but he always thought he had a much better relationship with Ayana, as the youngest of his sisters; they were closer in age and had more things in common or so he thought!

CHAPTER 9

Jamaica 1961

Ayana Wilkes was just three months old when she was uprooted from Jamaica and brought to England, much of what happened then was told to her by older sisters, as she was too young to remember or understand. As far as she could remember, she did most of her growing up in Jamaica with her grand mother as her guardian. She lived with her two sisters, Abigail and Maurita and she was told she had a brother called Dave in England, who she knew nothing about, born in 1966. The three sisters were shipped back to Jamaica in 1961 to live with their grand mother, Doris. Ayana was a year old. The Wilkes sisters returned to Jamaica just as the country started its political change from the old colonial style governance to self-governance.

Political Independence was granted in 1962, following Jamaica's rejection, by referendum, of membership in the Federation of the West Indies. Jamaica was given a Westminster style constitution, with a Governor-general as the representative of the British Crown, and a bicameral Parliament. There was a House of Representatives consisting of elected representatives and a Senate appointed by the Prime Minister and the Leader of the Opposition. The government was headed by a Prime Minister, who was required to consult with the Governor General and the Leader of the Opposition on certain matters. The main resources of the country were the mining industry with the production of bauxite and alumina industry as the main employer of the people. The girls were exposed to a variety of people during their early years in Jamaica, as the vast majority of Jamaicans were of African Descent or mixed race, east Indians, Chinese and European. The Europeans were mainly from the old colonial masters, Spain and England.

The Wilkes girls arrived in Jamaica by ship, they were picked up their gran, Doris who lived miles away from the capital, Kingston. Doris was from a middleclass family who made their wealth from running a plantation. Doris's dad got his freedom very early in the struggle and was able to negotiate the handover of the plantation from an English farmer looking to escape the country. The writing was on the wall that the business of farming was never going to be the same again, especially after the English abolished the sale of slaves in Jamaica. The plantation was located in the coffee growing areas of the blue mountain, where tourist beaches are a distant prospect. Ayana's early impression of the plantation was that of an idyllic heaven on earth, they were located at the highest point of the road going up through Newcastle and down to the Buff bay. Up in the mountains where the coffee bushes thrive there were a wonderful range of wild flowers and shrubs not found at lower levels. The almost over-powering scent from the wild ginger stayed with Ayana for many years, as did the agapanthus, angel's trumpets and eucalyptus. They were far removed from the pavements and city streets of Kingston; there were few cars and less noise and bustle. Ayana would spend many a mornings running around the plantation with her sisters very early in the morning, just watching her older siblings doing their chores before going off to school wondering how old she had to be before she was allowed to have her own chores. In the meantime, as they slept in the same room, she usually woke up just as Abigail and Maurita got out of bed, she would enjoy the atmosphere. As each day dawns, a beguiling mist gave way to the first rays of sunshine. The air was fresh, the breeze gentle and the plantation serene, like the calm before the storm. The tranquillity is enhanced by a constant chirping from the birds. Beyond the cliffs below, there is a bewitching view of the coastline, the sea with its delicate tincture and rhythmic waves. In the distance, Ayana remembers being able to see fishermen paddling their small canoes to cast their nets or raise their pots. As she looks westward, there was a panoramic view of the fertile plains, with the gentle streams making their way through the coffee fields. The surrounding hills were dotted with humble cottages where live proud but gentle people, farmers in the main, tending their crops. Gardens are resplendent with crotons, ferns and hibiscus. As the evening ends, she could see the sun, like a burning ball of fire; disappear slowly below the western sky. Ayana felt loved and at home with her family and one with nature at this spot. By age four, Ayana began to realise that her cosy little world wasn't as perfect as she first thought, her relationship with her sisters was always confrontational, it seemed they were always finding fault with whatever she did, sometimes she wondered if she was despised just because she was the youngest and the most adored, well she thought she was, by their grandmother, Doris, who said it often enough in the presence of her sisters. Doris would go out of her way to buys things for, take her out to the city or the farm market; she spent a lot of time reading, singing traditional songs. The songs, a cultural baggage of her past where songs and proverbs were used to make sense of their new living conditions in Jamaica and to comment on social and political developments in post independent Jamaica. Doris enjoyed a good sing song and extolling the virtues of her growing up in a world where blacks had to fight for their freedom from slavery and the daily grind of plantation work for the white colonialist. She regaled Ayana with stories of the struggle, the great war of 1914, the national movement and decolonisation, the people involved, the likes of Marcus Mosiah Garvey, Alexander Bustamante and Norman Manley. Ayana enjoyed her grandmother's stories, but she couldn't relate to them as the current world was so far removed from the one she experienced. Ayana longed for those moments, especially when Doris is gone all day trying to drum up trade for the plantation. The other sisters resented the fact that she was not yet able to do any chores around the plantation, they took out their frustration on her regularly. Even at this early age, it was obvious Ayana would take her fathers long lean tall body while the sisters were looking more like their mum. The other issue brewing was the plantations dependence on the money from

England, to start off, this was a welcome extra but as things became more expensive and the plantation's yield diminished, it became a life saving fund. Dennard and Mia tried to send money to the plantation every month from England but due to their own problems, it wasn't always possible. By late 1965 the plantation was going through a very bad patch and becoming more reliant on money sent from England by Dennard to survive the dry spells. The few times when the money was not forthcoming, things were pretty hard on the family. The closest plantation to the Wilkes was still owned by a white family, the Blackburne's, who had a son about the same age as Ayana. Doris had gone out of her way not to mingle or socialise with the Blackburne family, it was understandable knowing that the first Blackburne flogged Doris's brother to death not too long ago during the slavery period. It's a memory Doris has had to live with her whole life, the only redeeming factor being her success from being a household maid in the Blackburne household to owning the plantation right beside them. At first, the Blackburne's weren't best pleased that Doris bought the plantation, but later they came to realise that it was to their advantage that they knew the owners and that it wasn't one of the more radical blacks of the national movement who would have made sure they left the area. While Doris never socialised with the Blackburne, she also didn't go out of her way to publicize the fact that they were there and that they still employed blacks on very demeaning wages. The problem was that those employed by the Blackburnes were desperate and any political upheaval brought by Doris would have affected the workers more than the Blackburnes, so she bit her lip and let them be. Ayana becoming friendly with their last born, Clifford, was definitely not what Doris wanted or expected. She expected the Blackburnes to keep their kin away from hers. The funny thing was that Ayana and Clifford met simply by both of them being bored and running around their plantation. They had spotted each other on several occasions, both not knowing if the other would answer if they called out. Ayana was curios though, as she had never really had the opportunity to speak to a white person. On one of her numerous days out on the plantation, it was very late in the day, her sisters were busy doing their last batch of chores just before dinner, Ayana as always was left to her own device. She saw Clifford at a distance, on his side of the plantation running among the coffee plants, she made to go closer; looking over her shoulder to confirm her sisters weren't looking in her direction. She called out to him, and gave a tentative wave as she caught his attention. Clifford looked over at her for what felt to

Ayana like an eternity, just as Ayana was about to give up and run back to her sisters, Clifford's face broke out in a wide smile, and he waved vigorously in return. It was as if there was a delay between Clifford seeing Ayana waving to him and his brain telling him someone was waving to him. It was a couple of years later it was explained to her that he had a sickness called Dawn's syndrome, whatever that meant.

Ayana and Clifford had several eventful playtime on the plantations prior to their parents finding out, Doris did forbid Ayana from seeing Clifford once she found out but later changed her mind when she discovered he had Dawn's syndrome, Ayana couldn't understand how or why that made any difference, to her he was just a playmate, anyways, she's just a kid, what does she know. It seemed in Doris's mind, the fact that Clifford had an incurable disease, was good enough to absolve him of all his sins, including being white and a direct lineage of the Blackburne's

Dennard and Mia were just about settling down in England and they were seriously thinking about bringing the girls back to England, especially in the wake of the political situation in Jamaica. Between 1964 and 1967 Jamaica entered a phase of "post-Independence depression". The granting of Independence was followed by disillusion and disappointment as living standards failed to improve with a Jamaican government in office. Thus the late 1960's were mainly a period of social unrest. In 1965 riots broke out in West Kingston and many shops belonging to the Chinese community were looted. In 1966 a state of emergency was declared and in 1968 many public services went on strike. Just prior to the 1968 strikes, Dennard had sent funds for the girls to be shipped back to England. Dennard and Mia had two years with Dave and Dennard assumed Mia should be strong enough to cope with all her children. On their arrival in London, Dennard, Mia and Dave met them. Dave was two years old and the darling of his parents, Mia had a change of personality from the last time the girls were in London, she had more friends, she adored and dotted on Dave, she enjoyed taking Dave out with the other mothers in the neighbourhood, and she still enjoyed the occasional dance. It was a strange house that the girls returned, Ayana couldn't really remember much of her parents, but the shift of attention from her to Dave and the lack of her adoring grandmother took some getting used to while Abigail and Maurita, who remembered exactly how their mum was prior to them being shipped off to Jamaica were extremely resentful of Dave. They felt unloved and unwanted, thinking their presence caused their mother heartache and hence the need to send them away. They also couldn't understand why the presence of another kid in the house would give Mia so much joy. The Wilkes also did not help the situation by always cooing and behaving silly around Dave while in the same vein being very hard on the girls. Abigail suffered the most, as the first; she was tasked with looking after her younger ones. Her daily chores included making sure the girls had their bath, dressed, brushed their teeth and got to school okay. She was also supposed to protect them at school and on their way home. The strange thing in the Wilkes household was that the older you were, the more you were shouted on and expected to be good at all times, you were not supposed to be silly in anyway, that was the sole remit of the younger ones. Thus Ayana and Dave could kill someone, and they'll probably get a "oh, how cute you are" but in her case it was "what were you thinking of, you should be ashamed of yourself, you should be more sensible". The more that was expected of Abigail, the more she withdrew into herself, there was hardly any relationship between Abigail and Mia and Maurita barely had a relationship with Mia as well. Ayana on the other hand seemed to work or worm her way into Mia's heart. This was probably due to the fact that she tried to take Dave on as a playmate, there was no one else anyway and her older sisters were too critical of her and too busy with their chores. She was left baby sitting Dave and they would spend hours together. Dave practically learned to speak by copying Ayana. Dennard was no better than Mia when it came to the girls, he was oblivious to the issues surrounding the girls and Mia, he was too busy providing for his family, he spent so little time with the girls and was unable to relate to them. The strange thing was that he could have a conversation with Ayana, especially when Dave was around but could only muster the occasional grunt to Abigail and Maurita. Dennard was not aware of Ayana's penchant for making friends with white boys, so it came as a shock when Dennard on returning from work one summers day caught Ayana outside the house chatting happily away without a care in the world with one of the few remaining polish immigrants in the neighbourhood. Dennard remembered the early years in the street and the warning he received from the residents then, he quickly grabbed hold of her, dragging her indoors ready to give a her a good talking to. Mai looked at Dennard, all surprised, wondering what the problem was as Dennard explained to her what he had just witnessed outside. He had a shocked look on his face as Mia explained to him that Ayana had been friendly with the boy for a while now and that the boy had actually visited and been in their home. Dennard was practically choking from incredulity, he wondered if the boys' family was relatively new in the neighbourhood, and Mia said, they were. Mia met the family at the grocery store, well she met the mum, Katherine, and the boy,

What's his name, Ayana?

Alfonse, answered Ayana,

Yes that's it, replied Mia.

The mum seemed very nice and she was genuinely friendly, the boy was also very interested in knowing about black people, as this was their first personal experience. Anyway, it seemed Dennard had been so busy scrounging a living; he failed to notice his changing environment. He did however warn against complacency on both Mia and Ayana's, explaining the fact that even though some are happy to integrate with blacks, there will be the few who will hate the idea and they may cause trouble.

The Wilkes household continued with their lives with unresolved issues, which manifested with greater occurrence. Dennard and Mia couldn't understand why Abigail and Maurita went out of their way to disobey instructions; it was as if they enjoyed being grounded or having their lunch money withdrawn. Unknown to Dennard and Mia, Abigail and Maurita were screaming for attention, which they only received when they were naughty. If the instruction was not to stay out late, they stayed out late, if it was to come straight home from school, they didn't, if it was not to spend time with certain people, they did. This situation, as far as Dave could remember got worse the older the girls got. Dave remembers when Abigail got pregnant, that was a very bad time at the Wilkes. Abigail had been seeing a boy from college who Dennard had taken an immediate dislike to, he was everything Dennard was afraid off in terms of the new world in London. He was part of the 70's London crowd; always involved in some racial march or the other, campaigning for rights of blacks, on the same hand preaching for the right of Jamaicans to live the way they want to, as in being able to smoke their weed whenever they wanted. The boy was always in trouble. Dennard barred Abigail from seeing him and thought that was the end of it. It came as a huge surprise when Abigail announced one evening, right in the middle of dinner that she was pregnant. Dennard almost had a coronary; his face went all white, now for a black man that is saying something. Mia quickly intervened, instructed everyone else to go to their rooms while they discussed with Abigail. Dave wasn't privy to the discussion or what happened between Abigail and her boyfriend, but all he remembers is that Abigail had the kid, a boy called Jermain. He lived with the Wilkes and Abigail went back to school immediately after having him. Abigail was never able to keep a steady relationship; this was not for want of trying several times, while Maurita never seemed to find anyone at all. Maurita was pretty enough but she was too quiet and reserved, didn't really care too much about anything, boys, school, relationships or nothing. In spite of all the underlying issues in the Wilkes household, they were still a close knit family, but they were not prepared for the shock sprang on them by Ayana, who came home from university, promptly declaring that she was married and her husband was this white boy standing uncomfortably by the doorway.

This was the meeting of the Wilkes and Gary Chase, who at six feet was a very tall boy. As Ayana was over six feet as well, they seemed evenly matched. The boy was very pale though, even for a white boy, he had blue eyes, dark brownish hair, slender long hands and huge feet, he spoke very softly, was from up north, Liverpool. He came down to London to get away from his dying old industrialised neighbourhood. He hadn't seen black people until his visit to London, when he came to register at uni. Anyways, Mia invited him into the house while Dennard stood there motionless, gobsmarked; he had the look of someone who couldn't believe what was happening. The fact that there was a white person in his house was bad enough but that the white person is now a part of his family; he just couldn't bring himself to believe it. He went in with the rest of the family, walking in a zombie like fashion straight to his favourite chair in the living room while Mia took control of the situation. Dennard stayed, listened but still couldn't understand why Ayana did this to the family. In the middle of Gary explaining how they met and why they decided to get married without informing the family, Dennard got up and left the living room, refusing to accept the inevitability of the situation. Ayana wasn't particularly concerned as she knew she could always bring her dad round to her way of thinking, he just needed time to absorb the shock and to be fair to him, it was a lot to take in, finding out your youngest daughter was going out with a white man, or the fact that she was married to a white man or worst still, the fact that they had deprived them of a good wedding shindig.

Ayana and Gary looked good together irrespective of their different race; they looked genuinely in love with each other. After uni, they bought a place close to the Wilkes, a flat in Vauxhall; they spent time at the Wilkes whenever they could. The girls soon embraced Gary as part of the family while the men struggled to cope with him, Dave and Dennard found it hard to talk to Gary. Dave couldn't understand why he was reluctant to get close to Gary, but later, he would understand that there was a bit of resentment of Gary for taking the only sister he could relate to away from him and because of that he found it hard to put his personal feelings aside and be happy for Ayana. The more he tried, the worst it got, he would sometimes knowingly bring up contentious discussion topics just to make Gary uncomfortable. Dave would start recounting the days of slave trade or racism while the family was sat to dinner. Ayana noticed his attitude and she would go out of her way to avoid him. Their relationship suffered but Dave couldn't help himself.

CHAPTER 10

So basically your relationship with Ayana suffered not because she married a white guy, Gary, but because you were being a dickhead? Asked Baz,

I guess so, answered Dave.

Back at Park wine bar, there were now just the odd couple still loitering on the easy lounge chairs, most of the punters had left apart from a few stragglers and seeing how the waiters were giving us dirty looks, I guess it'll soon be kicking out time. Abe got up, made as if to go towards the toilets, but collapsed back down on the chair, apparently too drunk to move.

Right! Who else needs to go? Asked Abe, because I need a hand here or else I'll do my business on the chair right here where I'm sitting.

I offered to help, but he shoved my hands away, no offence mate, I'd prefer Dave, I wouldn't like for you to be tempted, especially in my state, as I am unable to defend myself.

Even though Abe said that in jest, it was hurtful, he was always taking jibes at me like that.

Dave said to me, ignore him, he's drunk, common, I'll help you. I'll bet Ade is the first black gay guy you have ever been friends with.

Dave pulls Abe up by the arm and they both walk to the toilets arms linked.

Are you offended when Abe makes those jibes? Asked Baz,

Not really, I guess I am used to it by now; it's been awhile since I came out and by now everyone more or less accepts me for who I am, well, those still talking to me. We've never really talked about your coming out and how it affected the others, especially me, said Baz.

The fact that I told you guys and no one went screaming down the road was a plus for me, it's not a very common thing you know, a black African British gay guy. I had visions that Abe wouldn't speak to me or be seen with me, so the fact that Abe still regards me as a friend is a minor miracle, he is such a homophobe. He also took my coming out as a personal disgrace as we are both of African descent. He is typical in his believe that such propensities must be a "sickness" not associated with African British, especially for one who has spent time in Africa. I was thinking how little Baz knew, as far as I could remember, I've had this huge crush on Baz, well, I should have said something ages ago, but I never did and it was too late now, I guess that's one secret that will go with me to my grave. Well, it was difficult, apart from the fact that I wasn't sure of my sexuality; I also couldn't see how I would survive such a confirmation within my community and group of friends. It just wasn't the done thing, a black homosexual person; it's unheard off, especially as he was of African origin. It's the type of thing you were hanged for in Africa or you had your genitals lobbed off and thrown to the dogs or something. On saying that though, it's more or less what has happened, I haven't heard from my parents in over two years since I came out. My brother isn't accepting my calls. The thing is that I thought as I was in London and my parents were back in Lagos, at least the so-called shame would be reduced, oh but how wrong I was. They heard before I got round to calling to give the bad news. I could never get that day out of my brain, I had come out a couple of days earlier, well saying that, I was caught snogging some guy in a club, so rather than allowing the rumours making the mill, I just blurted out in the office that yes, I am gay, so what? Anyway, after deliberating for a couple of days and playing the conversation over and over in my head a couple of hundred times, I decided to call my parents. I wasn't prepared for what hit me, don't get me wrong, I was prepared for the breaking of the dam once I had told them, but not for the onslaught I received immediately the phone got answered and they realised it was me. My dad was screaming down the phone, I could hear mum crying in the background; I was actually worried that something else had happened. Then it dawned on me what the brouhaha was about, somehow, somewhere someone had heard, there were rumours anyway, but they were told that I was gay and that I was snogging men. This was a disgrace, they didn't bring me up to be a pervert and they brought me up as a good Christian, what was the matter with me. It never ceases to amuse me how parents, no matter how old you are or how far away you are, still think it was their right to tell you exactly what you should do or not do, how to live your life and when to take a dunk or not. It was crazy, there they were a million miles away and my Dad was laying down the law, screaming that I would desist from this nonsense and get engaged to a woman pronto, they would expect to be invited to a wedding within the next couple of months. I tried to explain to him that it didn't work that way, what do you mean? He screams down the phone, you are either married or you are not, what is the problem?

Well, there is the little issue of me not wanting or liking the company of women for a start, there is also the issue of there not being a woman in the frame willing to drop everything and tie the knot within the next couple of months.

My dad then suggested that if the women are the problem, then fine, I should leave that with him, there were loads of women in Lagos looking to marry a Londoner.

At which point I lost my temper and screamed at him that I was not interested in women, I am in fact very gay, every inch gay and I have not been interested in women ever. Did he not think it odd that I never once had a girlfriend in Lagos? I asked, he spluttered something along the lines that I was too young then, so it was never an issue. This was despite the fact that most of my friends had girlfriends, anyway, there was no point discussing this matter over the phone, could I have a word with my sobbing mum?

My dad then said the oddest thing ever, are you going to give up being gay or do you want me to assume you are dead to us?

I must have stayed silent on the line for almost twenty minutes, the last thing I remembered was my dad shouting down the phone line after about thirty minutes silence, well, what is your answer?

To which I dropped the phone and went straight to bed without as much as a goodbye dad. I left it for a couple of weeks before trying to call my parents again, but to my surprise, their number had changed and I called their neighbours to patch me to my parents, I was told they were too busy to talk to me. You win some you lose some, which was my motto then, so I left it, thinking, they'll come round, eventually.

Dave and Abe came back from the toilets, flopped down on the chairs and announced that they were ready to go home.

I hope you didn't take my comments seriously? You do know when I'm pulling your leg? Said Abe,

Of course, I do.

Life can be so predictable sometimes and other times not, take for example, I never in a million years thought my parents would stop talking to me just because of my sexuality but I did expect to loose a lot of my black British friends of African descent. Its funny when you tell them, you could practically write a timetable by their reaction, the minute you say you are gay to an African black British guy, he looks shocked and then if he was standing close to you, he would involuntarily take a step backwards. This stems from an African superstition that if you mix with people who lean towards that sort of lifestyle, you could catch the bug as well. After that series of reaction, the next stage is to let you know that they are extremely into women and they want to describe to you in graphic detail their last exploit, so immediately you have to assure them that you are not interested in shagging them, it doesn't work that way. Then the last set of reaction is the not so subtle way of making exit excuses and then running for their life, it was the same thing with each and every one of my so called friends. Apart from Abe, I still have a few of my old friends, not many though, I lost more than I retained but I am not complaining. I don't know which was more work, those who stayed friendly or those who ran. Some of my remaining friends didn't know how to react or relate to me, should they talk about the fact that I was gay or was it a no go area as a topic of conversation.

Do gay guys play footie?

When you are having the usually boyish or loutish banter, is it safe to clap a gay guy around the shoulders like you would normally do with your friends, or will a gay guy break down crying of pain.

Do gay guys discuss nails, hair, makeup and so on and manly things like politics, football, cricket, rugby and any other sport going. It was a conundrum to my friends. I found myself having to explain on several occasions that I was still the same person prior to me coming out as gay; I hadn't suddenly changed into a girl or anything of the sort. I still enjoyed a good game of football and a healthy clapping around the shoulder like everyone else. My female friends weren't any better, those who had ideas previously of maybe someday going out with me now saw me as some sort of honorary girlfriend, while those who saw me as just a friend previously now thought of me more of a confidant, someone who filled a dual purpose, male, with the ability to understand female and hate males at the same time, God, it was a nightmare. Baz didn't really have a problem with it but Dave was such an arse. He wouldn't speak to me for almost a week, even though we worked in the same office, which was some trying times. I think it was Baz who eventually talked some sense into him and he then decided that he wanted a personal one to one with me to explain why I thought I was gay, because as he put it, it wasn't a black thing. He came round eventually, which was good for me as both him and Baz were my little helper in the office, anytime some pratt wanted to take the piss, they would think twice with Dave right beside me.

Those first couple of days were extremely difficult and Baz's support made me love him the more, the irony of the matter was that I practically provided Baz with his future wife on a platter. Things had settled down a bit at work and I thought why not have a party, invite a few friends round for drinks; what I meant was invite my last remaining friends round for drinks. Bounced the idea around with Baz and Dave and it was a go; we decided it would be an oldies night, no new music, strictly late 60s and early to mid 70s grooves. On the day my place was fairly packed, with beautiful people, I was very surprised with the turn out. My DJ friend was belting out the music and the drinks and chitchat was flowing. Dave arrives with Maurita and Abigail, Baz, sat beside me close to our DJ friend stood up to talk to Dave, Baz takes one look at Maurita and he was in love land. That was it for Baz he was hooked. At first Dave was amused by his childlike infatuation with his big sister but the more Baz stuck to Maurita's side on the night, the more peed off he became. I was getting peed off for a whole different set of reasons. I was just about reaching the level of confidence where I was about to declare my undying love for Baz, I actually thought tonight may be the night, you know, drinks, music, crowed and good food and here was this girl messing up my entire schedule. Baz spent the entire night holed up with Maurita, we hardly saw him. When Dave came to say goodnight, on the account he had someone to take home for the night, he still couldn't believe that Maurita was still chin wagging with Baz, anyway, knowing what Maurita was like, it would probably fizzle out by the next morning, at the most, a week. Well, that was the mistake we all made, unbeknown to us, this was the real thing for Baz, but he kept it quiet and away from us. Later we found out that he and Maurita had met almost every day for the next couple of months. All I noticed was that he was always in a hurry to leave after work, the excuse being he had to get home for his parents. Maurita had met Sobur and Eshal, Baz's parents, who were at first worried about the fact that Baz was interested in a Black girl, interested enough to introduce her to his parents. After Maurita had left for home, they sat down with Baz to discuss the situation. They started off asking what his intentions were for Maurita, to which Baz responded he was going to marry her.

Why? Asks his dad; are we short of nice Indian girls in London?

If we are, I can easily travel to Bombay for a wife.

Baz knew exactly which buttons to press, as he was well aware of his parent's humble beginnings.

Mum, dad, starts Baz, when you two decided to get together, you had several people saying it was wrong, but you went ahead anyway and you are still together, you have had a fruitful and blessed union. This is partly due to the fact that you both went with your heart; please let me do the same, so I can live a satisfied life as you have lived. That was way below the belt for his parents, and Baz knew it. That concluded the argument; he was allowed to carry on seeing Maurita and ask her parents for her hand. The only thing they requested was that if indeed her parents do allow Baz to marry her, they must have a traditional Indian wedding, that was non negotiable. Baz thought the easy part was now over, now how to tackle the hard part, asking for Maurita's hand from the Wilkes, especially after the fiasco with Ayana. But on the other hand, they may be pleased that at least they would have a traditional Indian wedding shindig to attend, one lives in hope. Baz decided the best way to go about this was to test the waters with Dave, so on one of our regular drink nights at parks, he briefly drops the clanger on Dave that he had been out with Maurita a couple of times and he was thinking of coming round to talk to Dennard. Dave almost blew a gasket, he went all rigid with rage, lucky thing he was sat beside me at the time, anyway, he eventually calmed down enough to rationalise the fact that Maurita was no spring chicken and Baz was his friend, the only exception here was that Baz was Asian, rather than a nice Jamaican boy, like those actually exist. In Dave's mind, no one would be good enough for his precious sister.

CHAPTER 11

After securing Dave's support, Baz and Maurita agreed on a date for him to come round to the Wilkes for that essential and compulsory man to man discussion with Dennard, Dave promised to be around for morale support, as if? On the day, he was nowhere to be found, Baz and Maurita were left to fend for themselves on the day.   They had decided to do the deed on a weekend, a very cold weekend. Dennard was a grumpy old so and so, but he was usually more grumpy and miserable on cold days. You would hear him sat in the living room drinking his Guinness and complaining about how God didn't intend black people to live in cold weather. The heater was on full blast throughout the entire house, anyone coming in from outside would immediately feel the oppressive heat. It was not uncommon for glasses to mist over on entering the house, if you were spotting one. It would never cross his mind to chill out on the freezing cold Guinness he drank, no! That had nothing to do with him being cold. On weekends like these, Mia, Abigail and Jermain were usually the only ones in anyway; Mia and Abigail would be busy cooking in the kitchen with little Jermain playing with his granddad in the living room. Dennard would sometimes go out to the nearby barbers shop to have a game of backgammon with his friends but he was always home just before dinner, you could set your watch by his punctuality. He was a man who enjoyed his food, nothing interfered with his meal and if anything remotely interrupted him, there was hell to pay. Maurita had taken all this into account and arranged for her and Baz to arrive bang on time when Dennard was relaxing with a bottle of Guinness in the living room just after dinner; he should be in a much better frame of mind.

The knock on the door was unexpected at the Wilkes residence, as everyone that was supposed to be home was home, Maurita hardly came home nowadays and David had his flat in Stockwell. Dennard, sat in the living room screamed towards the kitchen for Mai or Abigail to see who was at the front door, it was typical of Dennard, he likes to be waited on, hand and foot. Abigail opens the door to let Maurita in, Baz following closely behind, Abigail exchanged pleasantries with

Baz but informed him that Dave was not here, why didn't he try him at his flat? Baz grunted something about wanting to talk to Dennard. Abigail didn't think much of it and carried on back to the kitchen.

Hey Baz, how are you and what brings you downtown, Dave is not here tonight, I'm sure he would have been in earlier if he was planning on staying the night, the critical thing that brings him back to Brixton is his mothers cooking and since he's missed it, I can bet he won't be coming here tonight, said Dennard.

Baz, moving uncomfortably from foot to foot, arms behind his back answered, actually Dennard, I am here to have a discussion with you and Mai about Maurita. Mia was already in the living room like a shot, as Maurita rushed straight to the kitchen to tell her what was going on. Dennard had a confused look on his face, wondering what was wrong with Maurita, he had just seen her rush by to say hello to her mother in the kitchen, so at least she isn't dead or involved in an accident or anything, but, what was she doing here at this time of the night anyway, after missing dinner? He thought, knowing his kids, they only come round when there was a chance of a free meal. On seeing Mia rush into the living room and take up a position beside him, strategically placing herself closer to Baz right smack bang in the middle of both of them, Maurita was standing behind Baz while Dennard could see Abigail standing by the doorway grinning, already on her way to put Jermain to bed. Then the penny dropped. You've got to be kidding me, Dennard sits back down in his chair, feeling his age and totally exhausted,

Why? He says, I thought you guy's stick to your kind? Isn't there some nice little Indian girl waiting for you in Bombay or Pakistan or wherever?

Why would you want to be going out with my daughter, who if you hadn't noticed is black?

Baz, answered, Dennard, I think you have misunderstood my intentions. For a split second there was relief on Dennard's face, thinking he was jumping the gun, but Baz carried on speaking and you could see the relief on Dennard's face replaced by the initial pain of lack of understanding.

I was here, sorry I am here to ask you for her hand in marriage, we have been seeing each other for a couple of months already and we are sure of what we are getting into and to answer your questions, yes I do realise that she is black and I am Asian and no there is no nice little Indian girl waiting for me in India, I have never been to the place.

Mia interrupts, I think we all need to sit down and have a drink, Baz, would you like a Guinness?

I would prefer Jack Daniels and coke, if you have it, answered Baz.

Dennard exclaims from his chair, that is just perfect, a son-in-law I can't even share a drink with.

So how long have you kids been together and have you discussed your plans with Baz's parents? Asked Mia,

Yes we have and his parents are okay with it, they have also met me and weren't as horrible as dad is being right now, answered Maurita,

Forgive your dad, it's a lot to dump on him at one time, he would be supportive of whatever makes you happy, isn't that so Dennard?

Mia asked, giving him an exaggerated slap behind the head at the same time as she asked the question.

Okay, what are your plans and what do we need to do?

Mia, already thinking ahead of the preparation required prior to the wedding.

Well, seeing as we have decided to have a traditional Indian wedding, answered Baz, Maurita and I expect to pick up the tab but welcome any financial support going.   Traditionally, usually the wedding costs are borne by the bride, includes the decor, flowers, catering, entertainment etc. while the cost responsibility for the reception is the groom's family. This would be the only bit of tradition we will stray from, but on saying that, we have also agreed to combine some Caribbean tradition as well, where appropriate.

Mia and Eshal spent months together planning; Mia took it upon herself to learn Indian traditions and as much of the language so she could understand the proceedings. Maurita had to learn this as well as she was supposed to respond in Punjabi during the ceremony, she was also supposed to greet her in-laws. The girls were in second heaven; they seemed to enjoy the planning more than anything. Dennard and Sobur had a couple of drinks together, but it was stilted, especially as Sobur wasn't a heavy drinker. The only point of discussion that got really animated was cricket, especially when they described how they both enjoyed the games against England.

The wedding itself was a thing to behold, a mixture of two different cultures coming together under one roof. The Abhey's had made peace with their individual extended families in England, Eshal's family still believed Sobur was not worthy of Eshal's love but they were willing to accommodate him and welcome him into the family, anyway, they've been married for almost forty years now. As Baz is the first and only son, they went all out. Also, it seemed the older the Abhey's got, the more cultural they became, so it was going to be a traditional Indian wedding with all the works and trimmings. On the same hand, the Wilkes, as it was their first wedding in the family, went to town as well; they just like the Abhey's were becoming traditional in their old age, so it was going to be a Caribbean fest of colours and tradition. The wedding took place on a nice summer day in June, the day was researched in detail to confirm that rain was an absolute no no prior to confirmation of the date and invitations being sent out. The traditional wedding, Sangeet was to be held on a Friday with reception taking place on the next day at the same venue. The Mehendi was held at the Wilkes residence the Tuesday prior to the traditional wedding. Maurita, with her two sisters, Eshal and several of the Abhey's cousins turned up for the ritualistic application of Mehendi or henna to Maurita's hands and feet, she looked beautiful. There was dancing and singing, but not the usual traditional Indian music but regular soul music and pop, favourites of the Wilkes girls, as they were in charge of the music. Mehendi, the very name conjures up designs that flow onto the palm filling the young bride with romantic and expectant dreams. Mehendi designs are usually chosen depending upon the customs of different communities. The repertoire of designs often consist of geometric patterns, augmented and even eroticised by the addition of folk art figures of plants, birds, fish and other auspicious symbols. The fingertips are stained solidly with the red love juice of Mehendi, The application of henna is said to have a cooling and beautifying effect, it is supposed to soothe the bride's nerves, and at the same time give her a certain sensuality and stimulating power! A professional artist was brought in by Eshal to help on the day with the painting. On the wedding day itself, Baz dressed in his wedding attire, a safa sitting precariously on his head, rode to the venue in Vauxhall on a ghodi, which was a white horse, bedecked in red and white satin, with gold ornamentation, Sobur personally saw to the decorations of on the animal. Close to the venue, friends and family lined the streets, there was Jamaican steel band on hand and playing traditional Jamaican folk songs just outside the venue, barbecue stands with curried goat and rice was being served. The couple sat in the venue, Maurita, looking every inch the Indian girl, the fact that she was very light skinned made her look a lot like an Asian, as an outsider, you wouldn't recognise that the bride was actually black. She wore her sari like an old professional, after months of training from Eshal. The sari, a gift from Eshal was cream, with gold tips on the edges and the veil. There was a wedding cake, which was deviation from a traditional Indian wedding but insisted upon by Mia, it was a dark cake, it had been soaked for about a couple of months so the fruits and bread will be flavoured and moist, this was a traditional Jamaican wedding cake.

The tying of the Mangal Sutra or Thali took place with a hubbub of background noise from the seated guest. The Asian guests were not that interested and continued with their conversations whereas most of the black guest, who had never experienced such colours were listening intently and trying to catch every moment of the wedding. Dennard and Mia, sat at the front of the gathering were particularly pleased and Mia was reduced to tears when she saw Maurita in her sari. Maurita, seated over a sheaf of grain-laden hay looking eastward while Baz looked westward. The bridegroom placed the gold mangalsutra around the bride's neck. As Baz performed this ritual, the Nadaswaram was playing loudly to muffle any inauspicious sounds. This is called Getti Melam. Sumangali ladies sang auspicious songs. A turmeric thread was also put around the bride's neck. The knot, first tied by Baz, while the other knot was supposed to be by the groom's sister to make the bride a part of the family, a female cousin did this. Midway through the ceremony, Maurita changed into another sari given to her by Eshal, called the koorai, as a welcome into the groom's family. It was red in colour, the colour associated with Shakti. The women of the groom's family also presented Maurita with platters of fruit, flowers and candy, which they placed at her feet. On the covering of the sari, Maurita was given an auspicious ablution. It was a whole day affair with guest staying till very late. At the end of the day and during, you could see the proud parents; the Abhey's revelling in the coming of age of their only son and also their own final acceptance back into the Asian community. This was an irony, as they were initially rejected by the Asian community due to the fact that they married outside their caste, in the new world the fact that their son married a black woman wasn't something to make a song and dance about. Funny this world we live in, isn't it? The reception on the following day was a low-key affair compared to the previous days wedding antics, but it was no less enjoyable. It was a typical Jamaican affair, with Dennard taking the helm, everyone was welcome, invited or not. Rum punch, including a red sweet fruit syrup, rum pimento and lime was being served. Champagne and wine and spirits were also served. It was a generally festive occasion; Dennard tried his best to replicate the dance hall atmosphere of the 70s. Dennard found it an eye opener seeing every imaginable type of race freely mixing and enjoying themselves, Asians mixing freely with whites and whites with blacks and blacks with mixed race or those in-between and everyone got legless and arsed faced at the end of it all. All in all, it was a good day.

CHAPTER 12

Baz and I were up and ready to go while still waiting for Abe and Dave to return from the toilets at Parks wine bar. The place was virtually deserted now with the waiters practically waiting by the door for us to bugger off; they were practically holding the doors open. Two of the waiters brought our coats, just as we were buttoning our coats, Abe and Dave staggered out from the toilets, still drunk. Dave drops Abe on one of the easy chairs and bends to pick up his coat from the chair, Baz, says, well, your not going to leave him there, pointing to Abe, you might as well help him into his coat and we can leave, as you can see we are the last people in here and the waiters are not best pleased.

As Abe was closer to me, I pick him by the arms, he says to me,

I hope you didn't take my last comment seriously, I am sure you know I mean well and have totally gotten

over you being gay? I accept you for who you are mate!
Every Friday it's the same old story, one of us was so
drunk that someone had to take them home, drag them
into a cab and stop them from making a complete pratt
of themselves, it seems I am going to be stuck with Abe
tonight, at least I'll miss out on the dirty wife looks, as
Abe lives alone. His girlfriend of two years moved out,
implying that he wasn't ready to commit, until a time
when he was ready, she was going to live independently
and have fun, if in the process she met someone who
was ready to commit, so be it. Abe was hurting, as
he really likes her, her being, Nancy O'Connor, his
first love from Birmingham. After almost thirty years
of loosing contact, they bumped into each other at a
meeting between their companies. She was the solicitor
representing the company looking to merge with his
company he was the accountant. The strange thing
was that they both recognised each other at the same
time, it was weird and it was if they had never parted
company, they practically picked up where they left off
but on this occasion, they were definitely lovers rather
than friends. The lovers' bit was itself a major event, as
each one kept on putting it off, worrying about different
things. Nancy worried that she may have built Abe
up into something he wasn't over the years while Abe
worried about the fact that his philosophy of not getting

involved with white girls could be broken due to the fact that he knew he definitely felt a lot more towards Nancy than just mere lust. On the first day they met, they spent the whole day together, firstly they went straight to the office canteen and then they moved onto a local wine bar later ending up at Abe's apartment. They talked about the old days, they played catchup, they talked about their aspirations, they talked about everything apart from Nancy's parents and what happened the last time he saw her. When they finally got round to making love, it was two soul mates reuniting. Nancy had arranged to cook rather than go out to dinner one Thursday evening; she had a key to Abe's apartment, but used it sparingly. On the day of the dinner, she had called in sick, unknown to Abe; this was going to be the perfect setting for the perfect night for Nancy. As she got into the flat, she remembered how at home she felt the first time she visited. It was uncanny, apart from a few colours; she and Abe had exactly the same taste. The flat itself was on the third floor of a converted warehouse in Clapham. It was a three-storey building with views of the river Thames. On each floor were two flats exactly with each having its own dedicated lift. The lift opens right in the middle of the living room with old style iron grids protecting the flat from entry. Each flat had a special key to operate the lift, without the key, you were unable to get into the flat. There was an external steel fire escape leading out from the bedroom, this had a special lock on it as well, operated by the same lift key. Abe was a believer in minimalist furnishings, he had a feng shui specialist decorate and the only addition outside the old Japanese way of living was his electronic gadgets. On entering the flat, you were immediately taken by surprise at the size of it, basket ball court came to mind, with huge warehouse windows without curtains, the floor was reclaimed wood, there was one humongous easy black chair facing a 48 inch plasmas screen. Closer to the living room was his other love, table soccer and that was it. She took great pains in setting the place up as she was there by lunchtime putting things in place. The candles were lit by five thirty even though Abe assured her he wouldn't be home until seven in the evening. The food, pasta and a homemade cheesecake was done and waiting to be served in the oven, the red wine was on the table, left out to breath. Nancy had on a provocative, very skimpy red dress. She had grown up to be a very tall woman, long dark brunette hair, sultry eyes, the childhood pale skin replaced with dark Irish complexion which matched her hair perfectly. Her legs were long and slender, culminating in well-rounded hips with a very slender waist accentuating the ample breast. She was the perfect woman; god only knew what she saw in short stocky Abe. The night was perfect, Abe was relaxed, more than usual, as he didn't for one second realise what the night was all about. He enjoyed a good dose of wine and after the meal they curled up together in the living room in front of the television, candlelight the only other light in the room. Conversation between them was always easy and free flowing, it was never forced, well apart from when Abe got nervous when he thought Nancy expected a night of passion. To keep Abe relaxed, Nancy kept on reminding him she had a cab booked for nine pm; the driver would probably be pressing the flat buzzer any minute now. The atmosphere, the wine, the food and the conversation all added to dull Abe's senses, unknowingly, they reached a moment where Nancy's face was so close to his that he couldn't help himself, he lowered his head to give her a supposedly friendly kiss, Nancy was prepared, she grabbed the opportunity, gave him a long lingering kiss, tongues and all, that was it, relationship sealed. Their love making that night wasn't hurried, it was slow, very slow. They both took their time to take off their cloths, each watching the other very closely. They took their time to touch each other, softly, admiring each other's beauty, caressing, and kissing every crevice at the same time. They spent the first hour in the living room, prior to moving to the bedroom, it wasn't discussed, it was as if they both knew when to move on, they were like an old couple who were used to making love but were discovering each other again for the first time, words were not needed to be said to convey the next steps. Afterwards, they lay together in bed, spoon fashion, cuddling, not saying a word, neither slept through the night.

There was a raging battle being fought in his head, he spent ages with her as a kid, as an adult, he spend a good two years with her, he believes she is the right person for him but he couldn't or would not reconcile the fact that she is white, since he had always hoped he would end up with a nice little black girl for a wife. Therein lies the problem, Nancy fancies the pants off him as well, but she has waited for longer than any normal girl would have waited. I have the occasional lunch with her now and again, and it's obvious she is hurting as well and she is showing it, not trying to cover it up like Abe does with his male macho nonsense. Anyways, hope they sort themselves out in the end, they haven't seen each other now for over a month and if any two people were made for each other, it's those two.

Will Nancy be home to tuck you in, asked Dave, rubbing his palms together in an evil genius fashion, knowing full well that it wasn't the case?

Of course she bloody won't, answered Abe, she is probably off shagging some Irish boy as we speak, the stupid cow,

Hey, language, says Baz,

Common, you two, lets move it, I am getting weary of those waiters waiting patiently by the door.

Dave, why is it that you were able to accept Baz marrying Maurita but can't seem to accept Gary marrying Ayana, one would think it's not a race thing but a sister thing? Said Abe,

Me think you have enough of your own problems to resolve prior to poking your gob into mine, answered Dave but on saying that, Baz is my friend, it wouldn't have mattered if he was red, white, black or grey.

As we walk out of the double doors of Park wine bar and onto the street, the cold December air hits us in the face, removing any trace of alcohol immediately from our system. Dave looks around, where are those cabs? I'm freezing here. Battersea Park road was empty, with the traffic lights on constant green, the odd drunk or homeless person trudging through the snow; the street adorned with Christmas decorations, lights and carols still emanating from nearby homes. There was a light snowy shower mixed with a bit of drizzle, it made your eyes water and your nose dribble due to the sudden change from the cosy wine bar to the harsh cold weather.

You know something, you may have a point there, said Dave, in answer to Abe's earlier question, food for thought.

Guys, hope you are free next Friday, I want you all at my parents for dinner, bring your partners as well, I am not taking no for an answer.

Have you discussed this with Mia? Asked Baz,

Leave that to me, says Dave; I can wrap her round my little finger.

Well, the last time Maurita and I were at your parents, they were saying something about visiting friends for a party next weekend.

Not a problem, I'll sort it, answered Dave.

Just as Baz was about to protest, a car pulled in front of us, the driver, a Somali looking fellow, jumps out asking,

Taxi for Aid?

Ade, you mean, yes, that's one for us, I said, do you guys want to take the first one? Abe and I would take the second one and I'll drop him off.

Baz and Dave pile into the car and they drive off, leaving Abe and I standing in the cold, shivering, waiting for our cab.

CHAPTER 13

The following Friday I headed off to the Wilkes place in Brixton around four thirty rather than the usual haunt, Parks wine bar. Brixton in December is just like any other high street, gaudy Christmas decorations, shops trying to outdo each other by the amount of Christmas discounts on offer, streets filled with happy smiley people the only exception from the West End high street is the music. If you are visiting Brixton for the first time, you are stunned and overwhelmed by the intensity of the music, it emanates from every shop, every home and every car. The noise is sometimes deafening with the thumping base sound of hip-hop seemingly in rhythm to that of your heartbeat. You are afraid that if the music suddenly stops, there goes your heart. As I got close to the Wilkes huge house, I was taken aback by the number of cars parked on the street in front of their house. There were all sorts of cars, the usual BMWs, Audi TT, Mercs and the BMW Minis. The place was heaving with a cacophony of voices and music. The front door was open, as people trooped in and out of the house; I wondered if I had mistakenly come to the wrong address, Dave didn't mention anything about a party, he said dinner at his mums. I finally made it to the front door; fought my way into the living room to find Dave beaming from ear to ear with a date beside him, a girl from the office I couldn't really recall her name. It was a strange name, Cherri or Cherry, I never could remember. Cherri was a beautiful mixed race girl who worked in the IT section, I don't remember ever talking to her in the office but she was one of those people around the office you got to know their story. She is half Chinese, half Jamaican and half Australian. Her dad is Jamaican while her mum is a mixed race of Chinese and Australian origin. She was black with the Chinese slit eyes and long dark straight hair. Anyway, Dave had surpassed himself by making sure everyone was here. Well, when I say everyone, I mean every member of his family and his friends; no one else was allowed to invite their friends. There was me, Baz and Maurita sipping their drinks, Abe was standing by the fireplace with a face like a thunderstorm, glaring at Dave, the reason being Nancy was standing by the window, looking every bit as beautiful as I remember, there was Gary and Ayana, Abigail and her son Jermain, who was looking much older and more like one of those dancers you saw in a music video. Pants halfway down, hooded top, huge white sneakers on his feet, gold chain dangling from his neck and to finish off, there were a couple of rings adorning his fingers. Everyone milled around having inconsequential chitchat, Dennard the perfect host, topping up people's drinks and providing nick knacks. Mia was still busy in the kitchen putting the finishing touches to her cooking; Dave had provided help for her in the form of caterers, which was the compromise for her hosting the dinner party. The people I saw going in and out of the house were the caterers heading off after a hard days work which apparently started around lunchtime. She came into the living room eventually looking knackered, announcing that the table was now set and we could all head towards the dinning room for dinner.

The dinner table was exquisitely set, Mai went to town with her best china, I was half expecting name tags but she didn't go as far as that, instead she manoeuvred each person to where she wanted you to sit at the table. Afterwards, looking around the table, I'm sure she must have discussed the table sitting arrangement with

Dave. Dennard and Mia had both ends of the table, with Dave and Cheri to Dennard's immediate left; following Cheri was I and then Nancy and Abe with Jermain finishing off the left side of the table. To Dennard's immediate right was Ayana followed by Gary and then Baz. Maurita was sat beside Baz with Abigail beside her. Dennard lead the grace before dinner was served, Mia had a couple of girls to help bring the foot out and it was a typically Jamaican dinner, which I might add overwhelmed even me. There was just too much food on the table; there was Curry Chicken, Curry Shrimp, Escovitch Fish, Steam Fish, Oxtails, Stew Peas, Stew Pork, Tripe and Beans, Cow feet. As we all dug in and more or less destroyed enough food to feed a whole country, we were thinking now would be a good time for pudding, nah, there was then another round of food brought in by Mia's helpers that included steam Beef cabbage with either salt fish or Corn Beef and curry goat. All this while, bottles of wine, red and white was being served by Dennard; he made sure no one had an empty glass at any time. The table was also littered with jugs of different juices; there was carrot juice, sour sop juice, beetroot and sorrel. The conversation never stopped, there was never a prolong uncomfortable silence, the odd times when people were busy chewing and couldn't talk, there was eye contact and people smiled at each other, it was never uncomfortable. I guess the starting topic was a great icebreaker, which came from Dave. I was surprised he said it though, but the more I thought about it the more I realised that it was definitely the right way to start. Just as we all headed towards the dinner table, he started by apologising for forcing people away from whatever they planned for today and that this was something he wanted to do.

Dave said, I am sure you all had better things planned but I needed you lot here and if you are looking for someone to blame, please blame my friends who were responsible for me engaging my brain to issues around me and my family during a drunken night last week Friday at Parks wine bar. Anyways, please enjoy the food, mum has gone to a lot of trouble, even though she was hoping to be waited on tonight, so all please give my mum a big thank you.

We all smiled at Mia, gave a round of applause in her direction and thanked her. Mia gave us a mock bow and smiled back, she looked happy, the happiest I had seen her in years, well and who wouldn't in her shoes, her family around her, all seemingly doing great, none dysfunctional. She had the whole world at her feet. Just as we thought Dave had finished, we were just about to dig into the first round of food in front of us, he let rip with,

"God, I came in here today and thought to myself, is this bloody UN or what?"

After the laughter had subsided and some of us had managed to take a few tentative bites of our food, he looked directly at Ayana and Gary, who were sat opposite him and said,

Guys, please accept my apologies for being a dick head this past years, I realised it had nothing to do with Gary being white, but more to do with Gary nicking my favourite sister, no disrespect to Maurita or Abigail, but you all know I was fond of Ayana, it was an age thing, nothing more.

Ayana leaned across the table, reached out for Dave's hand and gave it a slight squeeze, Gary, smiled and nodded in his direction as well. Prior to reaching the table, Abe had stood aloof all night, sulking, while Nancy was the perfect guest, laughing, making a point to mix with everyone, small talk and a bit of flirting as well. Abe got madder and madder as the day progressed, he couldn't understand why though, was he mad that she was here or mad that he was happy to see her or that she was obviously comfortable in this gathering of mainly black people? He couldn't decide which of the reasons made him mad, but he knew he wasn't going to last the night if she carried on like this, she was doing his head in. At the table, as they were sat beside each other, he tried to sit there with a stony face but he couldn't help himself but laugh at the jokes and Dave's opening gambit. Nancy made a play of extending her legs under the table, catching his thighs ever so gently and apologising to him. Abe responded the first couple of times with a curt

Don't sweat it"

But the more she carried on kicking and brushing against him, the less he bothered to say anything, he sat there and just enjoyed it. Nancy had come with a plan, ignore him at the early stages of dinner, flirt with as many people as possible and then concentrate on him for the rest of the night.

When you came to England in the sixties, with all that was going on, did you ever think you would one day look around your dinner table, at your family and see such a wide variety of people? Dave asked Dennard.

No, answered Dennard, the thought that a white man would ever sit at the same dinner table was unthinkable let alone that I would have a white man in my family.

Let's not forget that you will or may have white and Asian grand children at some point in the very near future.

Ayana and Maurita glared at Dave but smiled sheepishly at everyone else around the table.

Dad, seriously though, the Wilkes family now represents the typical British family, where there is no white or black but shades of grey, so you should by happy in the knowledge that you are now a pioneer of the multicultural Britain.

Going on from our discussion of last week Friday, I would suppose that the term to describe every British citizen should be "British", we shouldn't classify it by placing either white, black or Asian in front of the term "British", said Baz.

Everyone else sat around the table looking positively confused at Baz, expecting further explanation of his statement.

I jump in to his rescue, well, the issue was, is it right for blacks to be referred to as black British, especially in an environment where blacks are so diverse. If we do decide to go down the route of "black British", then there should be another classification of Black African British, Black Caribbean British and Black Mixed Race British. In which case as can be seen it gets a bit silly, so rather than classifying the different spectrum of British, why not just refer to everyone as British. The notion that British inherently denote white, is now null and void, there is no such luxury anymore. All you have to do is look around this table, in a couple of years, the lines of colour would be so blurred that people will be unable to described which bit of the classification best described them.

Up until now, Gary had listened without saying much, no one, me included tried to direct questions at him and I actually avoided looking directly at him.

I personally think we have classified people within the country as Welsh, Scottish and English. To my mind, all we need do is add African, Caribbean, Asian and mixed race to that classification and we all remain simply "British" said Gary.

He said this without putting his knife and fork down, seemingly too involved in his meal to stop.

Well said, I responded to Gary's input, my thinking exactly.

Right, moving on to something less volatile, who's wedding should we be getting ready to attend, asked Mia, looking pointedly at Abe, Nancy, Dave and me.

All around the table, apart from Cherri that is, knew Abe's and Nancy's story, we could see the body language all evening between the two lovers.

Nancy responded coyly, well, we are all waiting on Abe to grow some balls and ask me to marry him.

Abe, not knowing whether to join in the laughter that erupted immediately following Nancy's response or be insulted, sat there looking all hurt. Nancy being

Nancy had control of the situation, held his hand on the table, saying,

Bless him, he needs time to confirm I am the right girl for him, which makes me love him the more.

Abe sat there with a stupid grin on his face, feeling all shy and vulnerable. Mia directs her next question at him,

Well, what's keeping you, there is a beautiful woman waiting for you to pop the question, stop dilly-dallying and get on with it.

Don't look at me, interrupts Dave, just as Mia was about to redirect her attention away from Abe, Cherri here and I only just met, we've still got a couple of months to know each other.

Then I broke out in a cold sweat as it dawned on me that I hadn't been to the Wilkes since I officially came out, they didn't know I was gay. Mia looked across at me, asking the same question with her eyes, the others waiting as well for my answer, apart from my friends, who looked positively embarrassed and looked pointedly into their plates.

Well, I'm sorry to inform you, that when I do get married, it wouldn't be to a regular girl, it would be to a man, if I find one, I allowed a short pause just enough to look up from my plate and catch everyone's eye before saying, I'm gay.

The table went silent for a split second, Dennard's face showing what everyone was thinking. Mia, the perfect host that she was, broke the silence,

Well, she said if that's what makes you happy, I hope you find someone soon; you don't want to be left behind.

Dennard got up from the table, excused himself, saying something about having to go to the loo, just as he was almost out of earshot, he turns around, looks at everyone at the table.

I think now I have seen everything, I do believe that things are definitely changing, some for the best others, debatable but I accept that things are going in the right direction. Ade, I will reiterate Mai's wishes, as long as you are happy, I hope you find someone soon.

Dennard continued away from the dinner table making his way towards the toilets, as an after thought, he turned round and asked a general question, not really expecting or waiting for an answer before continuing on his way,

Does anyone remember a comedy series called mixed blessings? It used to air in the early 70s.